Teaching American Students

A Guide for International Faculty and Teaching Assistants in Colleges and Universities

Revised Edition

ELLEN SARKISIAN
Derek Bok Center for Teaching and Learning
Harvard University

ISBN: 0-9662468-0-2

No portion of this guide may be duplicated or distributed without written permission from the
Derek Bok Center for Teaching and Learning,
Science Center 318, 1 Oxford Street, Cambridge, Massachusetts 02138
Telephone: (617) 495-4869
Fax: (617) 495-3739
Website: www.fas.harvard.edu/~bok_cen/

Cover Design: Ellen Sarkisian
Calligraphy and lettering: Ali Asani, Aviva Green, Zhonglan Guo, Judy Merhmann, Dimitrios
Trichopoulos, Isabelle Valadian, Namhi Kim Wagner

Photo Credits: Courtesy of the Office of News and Public Affairs, Harvard University, page
55; Jon Chase, page 29; Richard Chase, page 33 and 57; Duane Harris, page 12; Harvard
School of Public Health, page 80; Brooks Kraft, page 98; Ilene Perlman, page 10 (middle),
page 14, and last page (top); Barbara Steiner, page 41; Martha Stewart, page 10 (top), 26,
58, and last page (middle); Joe Wrinn, page 28 and last page (bottom); Laura Wulf, page 10
(bottom) and 36.

Published by the Derek Bok Center for Teaching and Learning

Contents

Glossary

Resources for Faculty and Teaching Assistants

Selected Readings on Teaching and Culture

Selected Readings on Teacher Training

Selected Books and Tapes on Speaking, Listening, and Usage

Selected Books and Tapes on Teaching and the Culture of the American Classroom

Foreword

In the course of working with faculty and graduate teaching assistants at Harvard's center for teaching and learning, I discovered that some teachers faced special problems since English was not their first language. More importantly, because they were not acquainted with the folkways of American students, they were not at home in the American classroom. These problems were very familiar to me because of my own experiences of several years' teaching in cultures that are not my own, in Africa and Asia. I knew how difficult it was to interpret signals from students of other cultures, and I discovered too late that some assignments I had given were inappropriate in the culture in which I was teaching. Consequently, I was very sympathetic with teachers at Harvard when they interpreted American students' questions as a sign of disrespect, when they felt that students in their classes were staring at them, and when they were stung by negative comments in students' evaluations. But I was also sympathetic with the students. One American student told me, for example, that he was puzzled by a teaching assistant's complete silence at the office door; the student could not decide whether or not he was being invited to cross the threshold into the office. I was even more disturbed by another student who said she dropped a course and was reconsidering her major because she could not understand her teaching assistant.

In the hopes of addressing such issues, a pilot program, "Teaching in English," was started in 1981 at Harvard's center for teaching and learning (now called the Derek Bok Center for Teaching and Learning). Expanded the following year as a result of an innovation grant from then Associate Dean for

Undergraduate Education, Sidney Verba, the program has continued to evolve.

This guide, *Teaching American Students,* is based on materials used in that program, discussions with foreign faculty and teaching assistants, and, above all, examples from their own classes. Originally written for foreign graduate students at Harvard, the guide was modified at the suggestion of several readers, by characterizing the audience in the title as "international" and broadening it to include faculty. Since other colleges and universities use the guide, I revised it to reach a wider audience. While adding examples from professional schools and including handouts many faculty and teaching assistants found useful, I also kept in mind the goal of a small, simple text accessible to people as they teach on their own. I recall seeing an Asian graduate student walking toward a classroom with a tattered copy of *Teaching American Students* rolled up in his pocket, the edges well-thumbed to white. I wrote this guide for him—to be small enough to put in his pocket and useful enough to carry around and refer to frequently.

While resources for teaching at Harvard have continued to develop—the work of the Derek Bok Center has expanded to include a full-time staff person dedicated to foreign faculty and teaching assistants—our efforts are not limited to that alone. Recently a requirement was instituted at Harvard to offer all new teaching assistants, irrespective of their linguistic ability, training and support early in their teaching careers.

A final word: I believe that, at any university where foreign graduate students are asked to teach, the adjustments to be made should not rest with the teacher alone. While faculty members and teaching assistants must be sensitive, students too should avoid narrow-mindedness that may verge on harshness in their evaluations. But the problem goes deeper. The following story was passed on to me by a colleague at a large mid-western university, but I have heard of similar stories elsewhere. My friend, a professor of Romance Languages, was sought out by a student for advice. The student wanted to transfer out of a math class taught by an Asian graduate assistant because the student could not understand his teacher's accent. When my friend inquired, he learned that the graduate assistant was born and raised in

California. While students deserve excellent teaching, they must also make adjustments and be open to learning from people who seem a little different.

Ellen Sarkisian
Associate Director
Derek Bok Center for Teaching and Learning

Acknowledgments

Many people's ideas contributed to the development of *Teaching American Students.* I am indebted to the many teachers—faculty and teaching assistants alike—who have discussed with me their own experiences of teaching and cultural adjustment, and especially to those who have contributed all the real (but anonymous) examples used in this guide. I am grateful to the following for their extensive comments on the first version of this guide: Ali Asani, Judy Bailey, Constance Buchanan, Jae Choe, Jorge Dominguez, John Fernald, Andreas Follesdal, Robin Gottlieb, Deborah Hughes Hallett, Ahamindra Jain, Michal Jasienski, Irene Kacandes, Margaret Law, John Maher, Virginia Maurer, Irene Mizrahi, Kirsten Moritz, Marlies Mueller, Robert Murowchick, Jennie Myers, Marcello Pagano, Heather Palmer, Jane Phipps, Louise Richardson, Peter Robinson, Ken Sasaki, Kathy Schneider, Doris Shiffman, Ben Wang, and Virginia Zanger. I particularly appreciate the contributions of Rita Bodlak and Cindy Moon, who handled successive revisions with patience and good humor.

The appendices in the revised guide consist primarily of single page handouts developed by faculty and teaching assistants for distribution at teaching orientations. To my own handouts I have added materials developed by my Bok Center colleagues for our work with different courses and programs. I would like to thank the following for their contributions: Terry Aladjem, Jed Dempsey, Mike Dyer, Daniel Goroff, Sue Lonoff, Jay Phelan, Judith Ryan, Lee Warren, and Mary-Ann Winkelmes.

Publication of this guide would not have been possible without the support of James Wilkinson, Director of the

Derek Bok Center, Barbara Hall, Assistant Director, and my colleagues who provide a lively exchange of ideas. I am especially grateful to President Derek Bok for his initial encouragement in this project, and for the grant that made the original publication of this guide possible.

Introduction

If you plan to teach and have not yet observed an American class, you should do this as soon as possible. When you do, you may be in for a surprise. Faculty and graduate teaching assistants from different parts of the world find much that is unexpected their first time in the classroom. Some of these surprises are welcome. But other aspects of the American classroom may be difficult to adjust to, especially if you are teaching for the first time and English is not your native language.

This guide is designed to help you adjust to the culture of the American classroom by preparing you for some surprises, by outlining teaching techniques that are expected by American students, and by presenting strategies that are particularly effective for non-native speakers of English. There is no single right way to teach. But, especially if your English is weak, you should quickly develop strategies to communicate with your students and to enlist their good will.

Many faculty and teaching assistants from other countries have language difficulties in the classroom: the students may have difficulty understanding you, and you may have difficulty understanding students, especially when they speak quickly, when they use slang, or when several people are speaking at once. This can be true for all teachers from other countries, whether or not English is their native language. Most teachers expect these difficulties. What they do not expect are other surprises. They may not suspect that different cultures have different assumptions about the academic background of college students, about how students learn, about the appropriate roles of teachers and students, or even about the fundamental purpose of a college education.

Furthermore, it may come as a surprise that many of their American colleagues take teaching seriously and spend time reflecting on teaching strategies.

American students, for their part, may have difficulty learning from teachers who teach as they themselves were taught in their own countries, especially if the style of teaching reflects radically different assumptions about teachers and students, learning and education. Problems with language and differences in teaching styles can be compounded by the reticence of teachers and students alike in approaching people of different cultures. You may not know how to talk informally to your students; they may be even more uncertain about how to talk to you.

Small group discussions at a seminar on teaching

I *Starting Out: A Quick Guide for Beginning Teachers*

"Be prepared for the informality of American students, but do not interpret it as a lack of respect for you. Do not take their manners (or lack thereof!) as a personal insult. And do not confuse their casual manner with a casual attitude towards their work and, more particularly, their grades."

—a faculty member from Europe

"Create a friendly atmosphere by introducing yourself: at the beginning tell your students that your native language is not English (even if that is obvious). Urge your students to ask you right away if they hear a word that they do not understand."

—a faculty member from Latin America

"Begin by telling your students (with a sense of humor) that you understand how worried they are to have a foreign teaching assistant. Laugh together with them and start from there. Be relaxed and try to break the ice. Get them to see you as a human being and not a strange-looking, odd-sounding person from far away."

—a teaching assistant from Europe

"Be sure to go in to your first class well-prepared. Know exactly what you are going to say and do. Before your first class, talk to someone who can give you advice—a colleague who has taught before, or a teaching consultant, if your school has one."

—a faculty member from East Africa

"See what the other teaching assistants do in sections and learn from them. This is a different country, a different culture. The sections are going to be quite different from the classes you had before."

—a teaching assistant from Asia

(For more advice on starting out, see Appendix: *The First Day of Class*)

Teaching assistants may be asked to be responsible for small groups of students at a class meeting that supplements the professor's lectures. Depending on the institution, the person responsible for the course might be called the *lecturer, course head,* or *professor*. Depending on the discipline, teaching assistants—also called *teaching fellows* or *course assistants*—might be responsible for *labs, recitations, problem sessions, discussion classes,* or *sections*. In this guide the generic terms are *teacher (instructor, professor* or *teaching assistant)* and *section*.

II   *Assumptions That Affect Teaching in the American Classroom*

What assumptions do you bring to your teaching? Are these assumptions consistent with the experience, expectations, and behavior of American students? What do you take for granted about the academic background of your students? What do you believe about how students learn? What has been your own experience of student-teacher relationships?

1. The academic background of American students

American high schools are very different from one another. Do not assume that college students have a common academic background. Unlike educational systems in many parts of the world, American schools have no standard curriculum and there is no single test for the mastery of a shared body of knowledge (see Glossary: *SAT*). Similarly, American colleges and universities have very different policies for admitting students. Some colleges allow anyone to enroll; others are very selective. Even in colleges and universities with rigorous standards for admission, students who lack what you consider a strong academic background may be admitted because they show promise to succeed. Because there is no standard curriculum, faculty members designing courses face two problems: figuring out how to teach American students and figuring out what to teach them.

Compared with students in other countries, American students specialize in particular academic areas at a much later age. While some American colleges offer programs with a specific professional focus (such as business or agriculture), many teaching assistants teach in colleges where students are expected to take a variety of courses that will broaden their perspective and familiarize them with the skills of different disciplines. Many colleges require students to take courses in different fields, such as languages, humanities, and science. Other colleges have a fixed set of courses from which all students must choose (see Glossary: *core*). The students in your classes may have a broader range of knowledge and interests than their counterparts in some other countries, but their depth of knowledge in specific fields may not be comparable. This is particularly striking in math and science: many of your students will not have achieved in high school what you consider adequate academic preparation. Many undergraduates complain that international faculty and teaching assistants teach at too high a level. Most successful teachers in the United States begin by trying to find out as much as possible about the background and abilities of their students.

Students come from very different backgrounds and they take courses for very different reasons

Strategies

• Ask experienced faculty or teaching assistants about the background of students in your institution. What is their age, education, or work experience? What are their reasons for attending school?

• Ask experienced faculty or teaching assistants in your department about the level of preparation you can expect of students in a particular course. What course material might they already be familiar with? What gaps in their knowledge and skills should you expect? Are the students freshmen in their first year of college or are they upperclassmen (see Glossary: *freshman, sophomore, junior, senior, upperclassman*)? Are they in a one-year program or a doctoral program? Do they have work experience or have they been students all their lives? Is the course part of a sequence? What courses are prerequisites?

"The breadth of education here is so surprising. Students can easily pick up on a new subject, even if they have never studied anything like it before."
—a teaching assistant from India

- Find out why students take this course. Do students with different backgrounds take the course? Is the course for students who specialize in a particular field? Is the course an elective (see Glossary: *elective*) or required? If students are merely fulfilling a requirement, they may not be very interested in the subject and motivation might be a problem.

- Ask your students about their background and why they are taking the course. On the first day of class (later if students in your institution are given more time to decide on their schedules; see Glossary: *shopping*), ask them to write some information about themselves on index cards. (For specific questions see Appendix: *The First Day of Class.*)

- Ask a colleague if you can sit in on a lecture, problem session, or discussion. (Faculty members typically give lectures a few times each week; teaching assistants typically lead weekly section meetings or labs in which students can ask questions about lectures, raise problems about homework assignments, do an experiment, or discuss readings.) After visiting a class, discuss teaching techniques and other concerns with the faculty member or the teaching assistant.

2. How your American colleagues expect students to learn

In the United States, students are expected more or less to keep up with the work assigned during the term, rather than simply take one big examination at the end of the year (or at the end of several years, as in some countries). To help organize the work for the students, the faculty member responsible for teaching is expected to prepare a syllabus, including a plan that coordinates lecture topics, students' weekly assignments, and the topics to be raised in class discussions or problem sessions (see Glossary: *section*). While many international faculty and teaching assistants view this as spoon-feeding the students, others are surprised at how well students prepare for class. Nonetheless, many of your American colleagues may complain that students put off too much of their work until the end of the semester (see Glossary: *reading period*). You may hear faculty and teaching assistants discuss ways to combat students' tendency to procrastinate. You may also hear about strategies for getting students to do their work.

"American universities have a much more open style. You can go to university on the basis of background in one subject and take a completely different subject. You can take courses, for example, in math, even though you haven't been your school's wizard in mathematics at high school. In many other countries that would never happen."
—a faculty member from England

In the United States, it is generally assumed that students will learn more in class if they are given chances to be actively involved with the material they are taught rather than only listen to lectures and take notes. The purpose of section meetings is to complement lectures by giving students the opportunity to ask questions and discuss the material of the course. Before coming to class, students may be asked to complete some specific reading assignments, to work through examples in problem sets, or to write a short assignment. In class, they may be asked to explain aspects of the material they are studying, to evaluate essays of fellow students or articles written by scholars, or to take positions of their own.

Many of your American colleagues believe that the teacher's expectations of how well students are able to learn affects how much they actually do learn. If teachers expect students to perform well, that is likely to happen. If teachers have low expectations, they may see poor results in their students' learning. There are many ways teachers convey their expectations to students, both directly and indirectly. Students sense when a teacher is indifferent or dismissive. Harsh or condescending behavior by teachers often discourages students and can lead to poor academic performance.

Students will perform better if they know exactly what is expected of them

Strategies

• When you give assignments, outline in writing exactly what is expected of your students. Faculty should be clear about course standards and the grading system. How are students graded? Are they graded on a curve or on a fixed scale? Are numerical scales or letters used? How much do homework and class participation count toward the grade?

What constitutes a failing grade? If possible, show students sample lab reports or papers that exemplify course standards.

- Make consistent, clear demands of students so they will keep up with the work in the course. Students will put off preparing for class in courses without clear, manageable, regular assignments. Focus students' attention on particular aspects of the readings. Provide them with study questions so they can prepare for topics that will be discussed in class. Show how particular topics or assignments fit in with the overall goals of the course, and how they relate to previous or future topics.

- At some point, instructors will find themselves in a situation where they suspect a student of cheating. Be sure that students understand exactly what work they must do independently. Some professors encourage students to talk together about their work outside of class. However, the work that students present as their own must be their own. The sources they consult must be cited correctly. Examinations must be worked on alone unless there are specific directions in writing that students may cooperate. Most colleges and universities have very strict guidelines that must be followed, with serious consequences for students if they are not.

Students will learn more through active participation

Strategies

- For each section, make a teaching plan that goes beyond simply repeating the points in the readings or lectures. Focus the students' attention and encourage as many students as possible to participate. For example, ask students to write a short paragraph on a particular topic and bring it to class; ask students to work out problems individually or in small groups; ask them all to bring in questions each week; ask different students to be responsible for different aspects of the assignment; or ask them to represent different points of view.

All students should have an equal chance to participate in class

Strategies

- The teacher's job is to teach not only the brightest, most articulate, or most experienced students; all students should have a chance to participate. If they are prepared to participate in class, all students appreciate having the teacher's attention. The ingenuity of the discussion leader may be required to keep some students from dominating and to include those who are reticent. Here are some techniques to try:

Design opening questions or activities that invite all students to participate. If students talk early in the class, they are likely to continue participating.

Ask open-ended questions that have several possible responses. This way you can expect several students to answer. For example, "What are some characteristics of an economy in a recession?"

Give students time to respond to questions. Do not call on the first student who wants to speak. Look around and wait until a few students have raised their hands before calling on someone. Look at students sitting in a part of the room where no one has spoken recently. Let several students (preferably in different parts of the room) answer a discussion question before responding to their points.

Plan discussions so that everyone has a role. For example, go around the room and ask students one by one to contribute questions; ask students to take turns giving short presentations; give students a chance to work out problems individually or in small groups.

(For examples of other class assignments, see Appendix: *Suggested Assignments for Discussion Sections.*)

Students can be very sensitive to criticism

Strategies

- Be polite and patient with your students. Never appear to criticize students with a sense of superiority, harshness, or sarcasm. For example, if your students surprise you with their ignorance of geography, do not say in a shocked tone,

"What! You don't know this?" Or, if they are unable to do a math problem, do not use the word "trivial." Do not point out that the problem is very simple or that every high school student ought to be able to solve it. Instead, say, "Let's take a look at the map." Or, "How about if we work on this problem together?"

3. The relationship of faculty, teaching assistants, and students

The professor is the person with authority responsible for the content of the course, the lectures, the organization of section meetings, and overall course policies. However, the professor, while treated with respect and usually deferred to, is often not regarded as an absolute authority who cannot be questioned, doubted, or even approached.

Some professors depend on their teaching assistants to be close to the students and to convey the students' view of the course back to the professor. Teaching assistants, as a link between the professor and the students, are expected to be approachable, available for questions, and responsive in helping students think and learn.

Most international faculty and teaching assistants enjoy informal relationships with American students and freedom of discussion in and out of the classroom. Although they may be academically unprepared in surprising ways, many students are bright, talented, and interesting to teach.

Students can produce astonishing work and can gain great satisfaction from their accomplishments when they are interested in the subject and are motivated to learn.

Students in this culture are encouraged to have an independent opinion about the material they are studying; in writing papers, they are expected to take a point of view and support it with evidence. Many of them will hold views about the material that do not agree with those of the teaching assistant or professor.

American students expect to be recognized, in and out of class, as individuals, unique and distinct from their classmates. (This is a cultural value that may be difficult to discern because, paradoxically, students also strive to be like

"The biggest shock was student evaluations. Students in my country would never be asked to criticize their teachers."
—a teaching assistant from China

their peers.) They may, for example, relate some aspect of a course reading to their own individual experience, as if their experience were unique. They will want teachers to appreciate that their thoughts and ideas are special. Yet few students would want to be consistently singled out as different from the others or favored by the teacher.

Students do not want to be prejudged by their appearance or treated differently based on what others may imagine to be their experience. Most students will expect their teacher to take seriously their contributions to class, irrespective of the students' gender or ethnicity. Students at many colleges and universities reflect the heterogeneity of American society, so it is risky to make assumptions about students' ethnicity, religious views, politics, or sexual orientation. Furthermore, Americans of almost any group resent the assumption that they are typical of that group, and most do not want to be asked to speak for the group.

Occasionally you may have a student in your class whose behavior presents difficulties for you as the teacher. Some students act so self-assured that they are arrogant, and others may act in a way that is genuinely disrespectful of you or their fellow students. A student may, for example, dominate the discussion by interrupting others; or a student may argue so forcefully that the argument seems to be against a person and not a point of view.

Students may not seem as interested in their academic work as you might hope. Do not take this personally. Young undergraduates value the college experience not only for the development of their intellectual skills, but also as a time of social and emotional development. For many of them, college is a major step in becoming individuals separate from their families. Their relationships with other students and what they are doing outside of class may be more important than their studies. Older students may have many demands on their time and attention, such as work and family. Furthermore, many students view college as a step essential to their future economic success.

"Many students don't come to office hours. Sometimes they come to speak with you after class when, of course, you are on your way somewhere, or they have only five minutes. You really can't have this kind of interaction. So, you live between the reality and the idea."
—a teaching assistant from Israel

Since higher education is not free in the United States, students (and their families) view themselves as consumers who expect to get full value from their courses. Many students will choose their courses carefully and try to get into what they view as the best class. Some students prefer classes with the most interesting teacher; others will stop going to classes if they feel they are not benefiting from them.

Students like to feel noticed and appreciated but not pre-judged

Strategies

• If you show that you remember specific comments that students have made or particular projects they have worked on, your students will appreciate it. Try to learn the first names of students in your class early in the semester and use them when you are teaching. Most students do not talk easily to others in the class unless they know their names. If you use students' names frequently, they will learn each others' names and discussions will work better.

• In exploring points of view represented by different groups (for example, an ethnic group or a political party), avoid putting individual students on the spot. Instead, ask: "What might an immigrant think of this policy?" or "What is the liberal position on this issue?"

Students want to feel that the professor is accessible and that their teaching assistant is helpful

Strategies

• Faculty members should announce their office hours in writing and should be available to speak with students informally after lectures (see Appendix: *Office Hours*) or through e-mail. Do not be surprised if students never come to see you during office hours, but many students welcome the opportunity to raise questions with you after the lecture.

• Teaching assistants should encourage students to meet with them individually. It requires some effort to get students to come to office hours, but both of you will benefit from this informal contact. Hold special office hours early in the semester; pass a sheet of paper around the class with times and lines where students can sign up. Offer review sessions before the mid-term or final exam. Talk to students informally during office hours or before and after class.

Find out what they are interested in and talk to them about what they are doing. In class, ask for their thoughts on what they are reading or specific aspects of the material they are learning.

Teachers can feel challenged by students' viewpoints or questions

Strategies

• When students express a point of view that is different from that of the professor or the teaching assistant, the issue may be worth pursuing. Students can be asked to provide and examine evidence together. Say, for example, "Can we take a look at the arguments for this point of view?" or "What are some reasons that there is real debate about this issue?"

• When students ask questions, understand that this is not necessarily a challenge to the teacher's authority. Re-state the question to be sure you understand it. If you are not sure of the answer, do not be afraid to admit this to your student. You can say, "I don't know." You can ask if anyone else knows the answer; you can ask a student to look it up;

A professor guides teaching assistants on grading

or you can offer to find out more information for the following class.

Teaching assistants are a link between the professor and the students

Strategies

- At meetings with the professor and other teaching assistants, discuss problems that your students are having with the material. Students in other sections may be having similar problems. Together, the professor and teaching assistants may arrive at common solutions.

All students must be treated according to the same standards

Strategies

- All students must have the same opportunity to meet you outside of class. For example, if you offer to meet students individually in office hours or for coffee, similar meetings must be available to all students. Favoritism or the perception of unwanted attention can have serious consequences. Most colleges and universities have written policies about sexual harassment and administrators you can talk to if you are uncertain about the meaning of the policies. (See Appendix: *What is Sexual Harassment?*) Avoid favoritism and the appearance of favoritism.

- All students want to be treated equally and fairly both in the classroom and on their graded work. Be aware of any tendencies in your own culture that may seem unfair to some students. For example, if it is considered inappropriate in your culture for a man to look at a woman's face, the women in the class may interpret this as excluding them from the discussion. Although it might be considered appropriate in your culture to grade women according to different standards from men, here it would be considered very unfair.

Students do not want you to let others know about their academic performance or their private lives

Strategies

- Most colleges and universities have rules ensuring confidentiality about students' academic performance. You, too, should preserve students' privacy. While you may tell students the range of marks in a class, do not reveal individuals' grades or scores to the class, or post grades publicly, even with students' identification numbers. Do not tell them who was ranked number one or number two in an assignment. Do not ask them to pick up papers in a way that allows students to see each others' grades. Ask someone in your department about communicating grades to students.

- Some students may tell you personal information about their lives, their aspirations, or their problems. Do not discuss with other students, in or out of class, information that you have learned about one of their classmates. If students tell you something about themselves privately, they probably assume they are speaking in confidence. If you are unsure whether a particular kind of information is considered confidential in this culture, ask an American friend or colleague. Americans may not be able to give you the rules, but they may be able to guide you on a particular occasion.

Students have lives outside the classroom

Strategies

- At the beginning of the semester give students a written syllabus that includes the dates of all assignments, papers, and tests. Allow students to plan their time. Be clear about the policy for late work.

Students volunteer in neighborhood schools

Participation in sports: one of many demands on students' time

- Find out the calendar of important holidays (for example, Thanksgiving) and extra-curricular activities (for example, sports practice and theater productions). You must also appreciate how the students' lives outside of class (for example, time spent on paid jobs, volunteer work, or stress over personal relationships) can affect their performance in school. This will help you understand lapses in their academic work, even if you do not formally make allowances for them.

- Be aware that many universities accept the observation of certain religious holidays that are not necessarily national holidays as a legitimate excuse from work. Consult with your department about these holidays.

Strategies

Some students may expect you to take more interest in them than you can or want to offer

- Some students are unaware that faculty and teaching assistants themselves have lives outside of the classroom. If you do not want students to call you at home, do not give them your home number. If you do not want them to call you late at night, tell them how late they may call.

- Some students may come to you with personal or emotional problems that you do not feel qualified to deal with (such as difficulties with writing, relationships with fellow students

29

or family members, or quarrels with their roommates) and you may wonder how much counseling to do. You may decide to be a supportive listener, even if you do not give advice. You may be able to suggest someone who can help the student, understanding that many students are reluctant to seek counseling. Many colleges and universities have professional counseling organizations, as well as peer-counseling services (see Appendix: *Resources for Faculty and Teaching Assistants*). University services typically include health centers to assist with medical and emotional problems, and resource centers to assist students with study skills and writing. If you feel that a student has serious personal or emotional problems, you should find out who is the appropriate person to notify in order to help the student, and perhaps talk to that person yourself.

Students may ask questions or favors you do not expect

Strategies

• If a student unexpectedly asks you an awkward question or favor (such as changing a deadline or requesting an excuse from an assignment for medical reasons), tell the student that you must think about it or find out about the policy of the course. You are not obligated to reply immediately. If you are the professor responsible for the course, you may want to consult with another professor or experienced teaching assistant. If you are a teaching assistant, talk it over with the professor or fellow teaching assistants. There may be standard practices or school policies for these situations.

• Similarly, if a student questions a grade that you gave on an assignment, you may think about it and consult with others. In some instances, the student may be raising a genuine issue of equity. While most teachers view these requests as a challenge to their authority, it is possible that you made an error or that your grades are not consistent with those in other sections or courses. After you talk it over with someone, you may decide that it is appropriate to change the grade. Be sure that you observe the rules of the college or university when you propose changes.

Some students can be very demanding and present problems for you

Strategies

- In some cases, students consistently push for higher grades. Ask an experienced colleague if there are usually many requests for grade changes in your course. The professor is responsible for explaining the course policy on grading. When a student asks for a grade change, some teaching assistants simply say that they will refer the request to the professor. Some professors offer the student the option of regrading the whole assignment, not simply the discrepancy noticed by the student. Most students are reluctant to take the risk that they might end up with a lower grade.

- If a student presents difficulties for you, such as behaving in a way that you find disruptive or disrespectful of others, discuss the problem with someone as soon as you are aware of it. Others have probably been in a similar situation before, and an experienced teacher or a teaching consultant at your school's center for teaching may have some useful insights. One strategy they might suggest is to talk to the student outside of class. Asking what the student thinks is going on and explaining the effect of the behavior on others may help solve the problem.

- Occasionally you may doubt that an assignment was written by the student who claims to be the author. Or you may question the student's use of sources. The professor of each course is responsible for announcing (preferably in writing) the course policy about working together on homework assignments. Colleges and universities typically have a written policy that is communicated to students about the serious expectation of independent written work in longer assignments as well as honesty in taking exams. Since standards regarding the nature and consequences of plagiarism vary, check on your own institution's published statements. Confer with others in authority before acting on such cases.

III   *Bridging the Gap: Approaching Your Students and Helping Them Approach You*

1. Do not be afraid to introduce yourself

If your students know something about you, your interests, or your experience, you become less mysterious and more approachable. Write your name on the board and tell your students what to call you. If your name seems difficult or unusual to American students you may consider a form or spelling that is easier for them to remember and to say. For example, a European teaching assistant named "Crzysztof" might decide to tell colleagues and students to call him "Kris" or "Chris." Most students address faculty members by their last name and a title. At some institutions "Professor" or "Dr." is customary; at others "Mr." or "Ms." Teaching assistants are usually called by their given names (such as Emily or Jonathan). If it is inappropriately familiar in your culture for students to call you by your given name, you might devise a solution that is more acceptable to you, without asking students to formally address you as "Mr." or "Ms." A Chinese teacher might say something like this: "My name is Xie Zhangliang [pointing to this name written on the board, then adding the easier pronunciation] but it is pronounced 'Shay.'" A Korean teaching assistant avoided the problem of what students should call him by telling them his family name. The students did not realize that he had told

---

"Names are very important in the American classroom. I would emphasize that you should tell the students your name and repeat it several times and write it on the board. Make them familiar enough with it so that they don't feel that they can't address you by it, because your name is going to sound strange to them."

—a teaching assistant from the Netherlands

32

An instructor meets with a group of students in class

them his surname, and the teaching assistant avoided the uneasiness he would feel if someone outside his family called him by his given name.

After you introduce yourself, tell the students what your native language is. A professor from Latin America with only a slight accent in English says that she always refers to the origin of her accent so that students can stop wondering about it and start listening to what she has to say. Early in the course add information about where you come from, where you have worked or studied, what you are working on here, and why you are interested in the subject you are teaching. Interject personal examples into your teaching, with small, incidental references to your own research experience or family life. For example, a Latin American lab assistant told his biology class what it is like to do fieldwork observing animals in the rain forest, and a Korean professor of design told about traditional homes having rooms separated by paper walls so thin that someone could moisten a patch of wall with a finger-tip and see through to the next room. It is probably even more important for international faculty and teaching assistants to introduce a personal touch into their teaching than it is for Americans, since the students need more clues to help them bridge the cultural gap.

2. Say something about your command of English

Enlisting the cooperation and goodwill of your students is the best strategy for helping them understand you. Tell your students right away that English is not your first language, but do not apologize. Reassure them that if you work together you will soon understand each other more easily. Say that you depend on them to let you know if something you said is unclear. One teaching assistant tells his students that, despite his imperfect English spelling, he does not want to avoid writing on the board. He simply asks them to be understanding about small spelling mistakes.

Here are some ways to talk directly to the students in your class about language:

"I am told that sometimes I emphasize the wrong syllable in English, so you may not understand certain words. I will try to write on the board as much as possible, but if I say something you don't understand, don't wait too long before asking questions."

"Sometimes it might take me a while to find the best words to express myself in English. If I hesitate, please bear with me."

"We may have difficulty understanding each other the first few classes. But if we are patient, it will get easier."

"I may ask you more questions than other teachers—and I hope you will ask me questions—so we can be sure that we understand each other."

3. Know your students as well as possible and be open with them

The better you know the individual students in your class, the easier it will be to interest them in the course material, involve them in discussion, and relate the material to their interests. It is up to you, as the teacher, to establish a relationship with your students. If you are unsure of your English, it may be difficult for you to take the initiative. However, you will benefit a great deal if you do, particularly if your English is weak. A Chinese teaching assistant with

---

"American students, by and large, don't speak foreign languages very well. Many haven't had anything like the experience of studying another language, so they're not as empathetic, I think, as they might be to the difficulties of speaking a foreign language. So my sense is if there's a prejudice, it's more one of language rather than xenophobia."
—a faculty member from Ireland

---

limited English reported getting on well with the students in his chemistry section after meeting them individually during office hours at the beginning of the semester. He had no purpose other than having a short chat, but said that afterwards it was easier for him to address his students and for them to ask him questions.

Some teachers are so nervous that they avoid looking at their students before the class begins. Other teachers end up with such easy, comfortable relationships with their students that they invite them to informal evening gatherings at the end of the semester. To start establishing a good relationship, arrive in the classroom before class begins, and talk to students informally before and after class. If the class lasts two or three hours, some teachers break for a few minutes half-way through. If the class is very long and if the students seem friendly, some teaching assistants recommend bringing soft drinks and cookies for the class to share. Ask if they want to continue doing this in the future, and pass around a sign-up sheet. When you see your students outside of class, greet them briefly and, depending on the circumstances, have a short conversation. Read the student newspaper, listen to the radio or watch television, and be informed about what is going on in the world so that you know what your students may be thinking about. Ask a colleague to coach you on topics of interest to students (see Glossary: *small talk*). Each time you see your students in a context other than the formal class and every time you view one another as individuals, you can help break down the barriers of role and culture.

Tell your students when you are surprised by their behavior or when something seems awkward to you. Do not expect them to change, and do not put too much pressure on yourself to change. Simply tell them what is on your mind. For example, a French teaching assistant was initially shocked by her gum-chewing, soda-drinking students who did not

"It seems to me sad, actually, that American students don't look at their teaching assistants as an opportunity to learn about corners of the earth that are tremendously interesting to which they haven't yet gone, but which are going through amazing changes and one might want to learn about through the eyes of a foreigner."
—a faculty member from England

acknowledge her presence when she entered the classroom. Finally she resolved her anger by good-natured frankness with the students. She told them directly, in a friendly way with a genuine smile, something like this: "Where I come from students greet teachers. I know you don't do that here, so I don't expect you to. But I have to tell you what a shock it is every time I walk into this room." The students' behavior

Teaching assistant leads his geology section meeting outdoors in the early spring

did not change, but she was no longer so upset; instead she and the students could relax and recognize each others' point of view.

4. Keep a sense of humor

A sense of humor can allow you to break out of your role as teacher and put you and your students on a more friendly footing. Your students will appreciate a sense of humor, but this does not mean you should try to tell jokes. A joke in one culture may not be funny in another, and it can be hard to tell jokes in a foreign language. Nor should you try irony. Irony can be interpreted as sarcasm, and students do not appreciate being made fun of. When you are teaching, you can tell humorous stories from time to time that relate to the material or you can give funny examples. But even more important is a sense of humor that will allow you to enjoy, together with your students, a shared moment that comes up spontaneously or a good-humored reaction to a misunderstanding. Some international faculty and teaching assistants suggest directing humor at themselves. For example, when you catch yourself mispronouncing a word that you consistently confuse, on occasion you could say, "Oops. There I go again." Or when you and your students become confused trying to understand one another, you could laugh and make fun of the situation, saying, "See, I told you something like this would happen." These comments can relax you and ease the tension of awkward moments.

IV   *Giving Presentations That Students Can Understand*

Teachers who are not native speakers of English often ask for help with pronunciation. Students often complain about the pronunciation of international faculty and teaching assistants.

Despite what you and your students think, pronunciation may be only a minor problem, but it can be one that is difficult to remedy. If you need help with English as a second language, get all the help you can (see Appendix: *Resources for Faculty and Teaching Assistants*). Courses may help your English; however, supplementing your language study with teaching strategies to help students understand you is also very important.

1. Write down words and use diagrams or pictures

How often have you, as a student, listened to a lecture in which the speaker develops a point about a term you cannot understand and have no idea how to write? The lecturer continues repeating this term. You write in your notes that "byfidbek" works in particular ways, and perhaps you even copy a few diagrams. It is only much later when you realize the term is "biofeedback" that you can make sense of the lecture and the diagrams.

To help your students' comprehension and note-taking, write a title and a brief outline of the day's topic on the board before class begins. Write down key words, especially terms that are difficult or that you often mispronounce. Whenever you use a new technical term, write it on the board. Give written handouts to your students. Use pictures, draw charts and diagrams, and label their elements. To make your explanations even clearer, point to parts of diagrams and equations as you talk, and explain these parts in precise words rather than saying something vague about the relationship of "this" to "that."

Examples

- A Polish teaching assistant in biology put the following terms on the board to let students see the list of topics for the day:

    —Relatedness
    —Haplodiploidy
    —Inclusive fitness
    —Hamilton's rule

- A Chilean teaching assistant in economics offered his students a more elaborate variation of a class outline. After he and a colleague discovered that students were transferring out of their classes, they decided to work together preparing a page of notes on the day's material. The handout was distributed at the beginning of each class. Students were then free to listen carefully and simply add to the notes from time to time.

- An English lecturer showed the difference between traditional medicine and high technology hospital care by opening her presentation with two contrasting images. One was a Norman Rockwell painting of a family doctor visiting a child at home, talking to the child at his bedside. The other was a photograph of a patient in a hospital bed surrounded by six specialists, each in a white coat looking at a different piece of equipment but not looking at the patient.

- A Korean teaching assistant in economics, drew a graph on the chalkboard representing the relationship of supply and demand curves. He avoided a vague explanation, such as "when this goes up, this goes down," by saying exactly what the graph demonstrated: "When the supply of wheat began to increase here in 19—..."

2. Use verbal signals when you speak

Most effective speakers of English use words to signal what they are about to do. For example, when they are beginning a class, they may say something like: "I think it's time for us to begin." Then they begin the class. These cues establish expectations for the listeners before the speaker actually states anything. Similarly, the most effective teachers provide a context before they begin teaching, linking the day's material to the previous class or showing how it fits into a broader structure. Your teaching will be clearer if you outline in general what you are going to say at the beginning of each topic, then explain the material in greater detail, and then summarize at the end of each topic. An often-quoted guide is that good teachers say what they are going to say; then they say it; then they tell you what they said. Verbal cues used at the beginning of a presentation and along the way are like a map to remind students where they are in the overall structure of the presentation. They also emphasize what is especially important or difficult, signal a change in topic, or let listeners know that the presentation is about to end. Verbal cues offer the added advantage of recapturing the attention of students whose minds have wandered by letting them know where you are so that they can easily begin listening again.

Examples

- Set a context for what you are going to say:
  "Today's topic is another example of..."
  "In the last class we examined...Today we will spend the first half of class on...and then we will turn to..."
  "Before going on to the next point, let me give one more example."
  "Those are the three basic concepts, now let's look at the first one in detail."
  "Let's reflect on what we have established so far..."
  "Now let's examine a contrasting example of...before we end."

- Provide emphasis:
  "It's important to emphasize, at this point,..."
  "This is the most crucial step in the process..."

40

"Just to underline this for you, the professor's point in the lecture was…"

"The message of yesterday's lecture was that it's more important to…So that's the whole point."

3. Use specific examples

Give specific examples as often as possible to illustrate ideas. Use familiar examples that students can relate to their own experiences. Bring in objects to make your points more vivid or use objects or data readily available in the classroom.

Examples

- A Norwegian teaching assistant rolled an apple across the table to begin a discussion about justice. He asked, "If we had only one apple to share among us, how might we go about doing it? On what basis might we decide who gets how much?"

Other ways to be specific include drawing examples from the class to demonstrate a concept or formula, and using personal stories to illustrate an idea.

- An Italian professor used students' ages as data to demonstrate a point in a statistics class.

Student demonstrates conservation of angular momentum

• A teaching assistant from a primarily Muslim country illustrated the tension between modernism and tradition by talking about the embarrassment a daughter might feel in walking down the street with her mother who was wearing a black veil.

4. Say the same thing in a few different ways and avoid jargon

Explaining technical terms in plain English is essential. The jargon of your discipline may be familiar to you, but this technical vocabulary can be especially difficult for your students to understand. The terms that are least familiar to your students are the very ones that you are most likely to mispronounce in English. This may seem surprising, but if you have been in the habit of using English technical terms when you speak your own language, you are likely to bring that language's pronunciation and intonation to these terms when you use them in English. Use plain English whenever you can. Write on the board, and repeat yourself.

Repetition can help to slow your pace and improve your students' comprehension. If you say things only once, the information might go by too fast for students to catch it. Furthermore, using different terms to express the same idea can help more students understand the material. This can be challenging for non-native speakers. It is difficult enough to figure out how to say something once in a foreign language, let alone a second or a third way.

Examples

• In a lecture, a European professor of physics used common language before introducing a technical term:

"Today we'll just consider fluids that are not moving. This is called hydrostatics."

In the same lecture the professor characterized the relationship of pressure and density in a variety of ways:

"The density of a fluid depends on the temperature and the pressure. A balloon, one liter of water...I try to compress it. It will be nearly impossible to get a higher density. You have to exert exceedingly large pressure on the water in order to get a higher density. These atoms and molecules are already quite tightly packed. You can't get a higher density."

• A Greek teaching assistant in chemistry used both repetition and non-technical language to clarify a chemical reaction. Many teachers might simply have written the reaction on the board, and proceeded to work it out. Others might have repeated the symbols out loud:

$$C\ (s) + H2O\ (g) \rightleftarrows C\ O\ (g) + H2(g)$$

Instead, this teaching assistant from Greece began by saying:

"O.K. Let's go to a problem that you should be more familiar with, that has much more to do with equilibrium." Then as he wrote the reaction on the board, he gave the following explanation in words:

"In the gasification of coal, an important endothermic reaction, we have carbon (solid) plus water (gas) yields carbon monoxide and hydrogen (gas)."

"O.K. We have this reaction. The reaction lies heavily to the left. I'm going to give you five different sets of conditions. Let's say this reaction is at equilibrium, and I'm going to perturb equilibrium and you're going to tell me what will happen to the amount of hydrogen produced. What will happen if…?"

• A Polish teaching assistant in biology helped students learn to interpret the results of an experiment. He used repetition as he described the data displayed on a screen:

"O.K., so this is our data set. Five treatments—control is also a treatment; sucrose, glucose plus fructose, fructose, and glucose. Now, how could we analyze this? Which means, how could we say there is variation among groups?" [students murmur different responses]

"In other words, are the treatments significantly different? Do the treatments matter? Do they change anything in the performance in, say, growth of—for example, aphids that are reared under those different treatments?"

5. Keep lines of communication open

Even under the best circumstances there are many opportunities for miscommunication. Ask a lot of questions, and follow up students' responses by asking them to restate ideas in other terms, to explain further, and to provide examples. You can minimize misunderstanding by inviting students at the first class to let you know when they do not understand you, and by not appearing annoyed when they ask questions.

Because it is often difficult for students to frame questions about ideas they do not understand, one of the biggest problems faced by any instructor is to understand what a student is asking. This problem is compounded for instructors teaching in a language that is not their own. You may feel embarassed when you do not understand a student's question, or you may answer a question that is different from what the student is asking. If you are not sure that you understand the question being asked, you can restate the question in different terms to clarify the meaning, or you can suggest a specific example to see if you understand what the student intended. Students' questions (and answers) will let you know how well they are following the class and how to adjust your pace.

Example
- The biology teaching assistant from Poland engaged students in an interactive presentation:

Teaching Assistant: So, there's clearly variation within groups and variation among groups. What is our null hypothesis? Could you specify the null hypothesis?
Students: [several answers] There's no difference between treatments.
Teaching Assistant: There's no difference among treatments. That is, no matter what the treatment is, aphids should grow at the same rate.
Student: And there's no difference in growth for those other treatments.
Teaching Assistant: O.K., and how would you…?
Student: You give the F-test.
Teaching Assistant: The F-test would…
Student: Wouldn't work. I mean, it wouldn't be significant.
Teaching Assistant: "Wouldn't be significant" means would look like what?
Students: [several answers]…would be close.
Teaching Assistant: Close to what? [and so on]

- When you want to ask students to rephrase in order to clarify or ask for a specific example, you can say:
  "Sorry, I didn't understand the question. Would you please rephrase it?"
  "Could you say that in other words?"
  "What do you mean by…?"
  "What would that look like?"
  "What would be an example of…?"

- When you want to restate a question or statement for clarification:
  "Let me try to answer what I think you are asking..."
  "If I understand you correctly,…"
  "What you are saying is… Is that right?"
  "If I read you right…"
  "Do you mean that…"
  "You seem to be saying…"
  "In other words…"

- Suggesting a specific example:
  "Do you mean that if…"
  "Would this [specify] be an example of what you are asking?"

- When you want to tell a student that an answer is unrelated or wrong:
  "Yes, that applies to such and such, but in this case that won't work..."
  "Yes, but what's going on here?"
  "Well, how can that be true if x and y are the case?"
  "That's what people thought for a long time. But remember... And now we know that's not true."

"In China, students don't ask as many questions as American students do. I guess the American students are more active in that sense. Here it's a good thing to ask questions and think for yourself."
—a teaching assistant from China

V   *Leading a Discussion: Providing Direction and Continuity*

1. Plan questions carefully

Because discussions are unpredictable, many teachers think they do not need to prepare. However, it is difficult for most people to lead a discussion effectively without preparing carefully ahead of time. In addition to writing down the topics you hope to cover and the approximate amount of time to devote to each, also write the precise wording of several questions you might actually ask. Imagine some responses that your students might give, and then you can see if your questions seem promising. Questions that are genuinely interesting, relatively concrete, and with several possible answers or perspectives are good to ask at the beginning of discussions because they involve little risk on the part of students, and many students will have a chance to speak. Questions with a single right answer offer little to generate discussion. Questions that are very complicated or very abstract are likely to get the class off to a slow start. If students know ahead of time what topics to think about they will be better prepared to speak in class. However, avoid opening a class with a study question stated in its most complex or comprehensive form. Instead, ask a series of questions moving from the more concrete to the abstract.

"I was astonished to see everyone sitting around a table discussing things. The professor is open to discussion and did not assume that what you were saying was wrong. What you say might even be right!"
—a teaching assistant from Italy

Examples

- In a class on the Japanese economy, the following question was given to students by the professor at the lecture so they could think about it before the discussion meetings:

  "Would you rather be a Japanese person working in an American company, or an American working in a Japanese company? Why?"

  Students had time to prepare, the question was broad enough for many students to answer easily, and the answers raised in concrete terms many of the general points characterizing Japanese companies.

- Other questions that can stimulate discussion include visual images and personal reactions to the readings.

  A Chinese teaching assistant asked his literature class: "What are some recurring images and metaphors in Yeats's poems?" A Korean teaching assistant in anthropology asked the following question after students read about a group living in New Guinea: "What are some practices among the Dani that you find hard to understand either morally or socially?"

- Study questions in their unedited form may be too complex or abstract to start the discussion. A question like the following is very useful in helping students prepare for class, but it should be broken down into smaller units to be useful as a discussion question:

  "Consider the relationship between Kawabata's *Seven Very Short Stories* and *Snow Country*. Is there a continuity of theme and/or execution? Do you see parallels between the works in their mode of presentation and style? Think about the revelation of the characters' personalities and the types of incidents into which the author thrusts them."

To break down this complex study question, you might begin with a specific, open-ended question such as: "Let's look at some of the characters in *Seven Very Short Stories* and *Snow Country*. What types of situations do they find themselves in?"

2. Listen to your students and encourage them

Some signs of a good discussion, apart from the preparation of the students and teacher, include broad student participation and an atmosphere of goodwill. The discussion is not for the benefit of the most aggressive students alone. You can create an atmosphere that encourages people to take a stand or express unpopular positions. You, as leader, can ask students to elaborate on points; you can include and support more hesitant speakers. If you use students' names and credit individuals for their contribution to the class, they will know you are listening and will feel encouraged. Conversely, when students' suggestions are off the mark, those students should be allowed to accept others' lines of reasoning and change positions without losing dignity. If you disagree with students, you can be polite about it; you can even be polite about answers that are just plain wrong. If you state your disagreement in terms of the idea rather than the student, it will seem less personally critical.

Examples

- Praising the right answer:
  "Yes."
  "Very good."
  "Right on the mark."
  "Did everyone hear what Jim just said?"

- Giving students credit for intellectual leadership:
  "Allison is rightly reminding us of a point of view we have neglected."
  "Thank you, John, for bringing this out."

- Showing enthusiasm:
  "Really good point, Susan."
  "Let's look at the issue Bill raised."

- Encouraging students to explain further:
  "Could you say a bit more about that?"
  "What else?"
  "Would you elaborate on that?"
  "Would you spell that out?"

- Encouraging non-participants:
  "Could someone give another example of…?"
  "Would someone like to add to that?"

- Using names:
  "Larry raised an interesting point. Maria, you had said something about that earlier. Would you like to add something?"
  "There's another point that relates to the issue that Jane brought up."
  "In other words, you agree [disagree] with Richard's point?"
  "In other words, what Joe is saying is…"
  "I'd like to add to Sarah's point…"

- Giving validity to an unpopular position:
  "This is an issue that most scholars can't agree on, so let's examine the point of view you just raised."
  "Many people might disagree with what you just said. But let's look at your basis for thinking that."
  "You have just outlined the argument of the minority opinion of the Supreme Court."

- Disagreeing somewhat:
  "Part of what you say is true. The other part, however, is not …"
  "Nevertheless,…"
  "All the same,…"
  "Still,…"
  "Keeping in mind…"
  "When you consider…"
  "A counter-example would be…."
  "I'm not so certain that…"
  "I'm not sure that…"
  "I really wonder…"
  "Even if that is so…"

"An exception to that is…"
"Another way to look at this is…"

- Disagreeing completely (but politely):
"If I understand you correctly, I don't think that is really related."
"I understand what you are saying, but when I consider **x** it leads me to **y** as the conclusion."
"I can't see how…"
"I can't agree that…"
"I'm afraid I must disagree."

3. Keep the discussion focused

To give students a sense of coherence, link ideas together to show their relationship. Gently interrupt speakers who dominate, and do not confuse students' ease of speaking with knowledge of the subject. Some international faculty and teaching assistants are surprised when they discover that some students may seem articulate, even when they do not know what they are talking about. Ask students to be specific if they are speaking in generalities; steer speakers whose points are tangential; redirect the focus of the discussion when their comments are irrelevant. Move on to the next topic when it seems appropriate.

Examples

- Linking:
"That would be another example of Martha's point…"
"That's the second reason why…"
"So you somewhat disagree with…"

- Steering speakers to make predictions or state reasons:
"That should result in…"
"Then we should expect…"
"That would indicate…"
"The reason why…"
"That brings us to the next point…"

"In many other cultures, certainly my own, you don't say anything unless you know exactly what you are talking about. But that isn't so much the case here."
—*a faculty member from Ireland*

- Interrupting politely:
  "By the way,…"
  "Excuse me for interrupting, but could you give an example of…"
  "May I add something here?"
  "May I ask a question?"

- Redirecting discussion after an interruption or digression:
  "O.K., to get back to the issue of …"
  "Let's go back to the important issue raised 10 minutes ago…"
  "To get back to the original question,…"

- Interrupting a speaker who goes on too long:
  "Let's stop right there and focus on…[picking up one of the ideas]"
  "Good example. Can someone else give another example of…"
  "What you just said is very interesting [important, etc.] and that raises the next issue of [turn to someone else and ask a question]"

- Preparing to summarize and move on:
  "Consequently,…"
  "Therefore,…"
  "To sum up,…"
  "All in all,…"
  "Just one more comment before we move on,…"
  "There's another point that relates to this issue that we haven't considered yet…"
  "O.K., we have completed [topic] and now we need to…"
  "Well, moving on to the next issue…"

4. Be aware of silences

We all differ in the amount of silence we can comfortably tolerate, but teachers must remember that it takes time for students to think. After asking a question—wait, look around, then rephrase the question and wait again before calling on someone or answering it yourself.

The most awkward silence is the silence following a difficult question addressed to you. Complete silence will puzzle your students, so you must show that you are hesitating while you figure out how to explain something, even if you simply say "hmm…" and nod. However, if you do not know the answer, say that you do not. Perhaps ask if someone else knows or say that you will look it up (and then do so).

Examples

- Rephrasing questions:
  If your question "What is going on in this text?" is followed by a silence of several seconds, you can move from the general to the concrete by saying, for example, "Let's try to get at this another way. What might Levi-Strauss mean by 'cultural-coding' in this paragraph?"

- Offering a choice after a general question:
  "This is a 'trivia' question. Approximately how much of the ocean is salt?... Is it, say, less than or more than 5% by weight?"

- Expressing hesitation before saying something:
  "Well, let's see…"
  "What I would say is…"
  "Well, let me think for a minute how to put this…"

- Not knowing how to respond:
  "Hmm… I'm not sure of the best way to respond to that just now. Can we come back to that later?"
  "I was wondering the same thing."
  "I really don't know what to say about that."
  "I'm at a loss as to what to say."
  "Hmm…I'll have to think about that."
  "Tough question! How should we go about finding an answer to this?"

- Responding to someone whose contribution impresses you but leaves you with little to add:
  "That's interesting. I never thought about it that way."
  "That's exactly what I was going to say!"

VI   *Understanding Meanings Beyond Words*

1. Body language

Your facial expressions, the gestures you make, and the way you sit, stand, or move can convey—intentionally or unintentionally—interest in your subject and students, an appropriate level of self-confidence, lack of confidence, or indifference toward students. Similarly, the way your students sit can convey—intentionally or unintentionally—interest and attention, willingness to speak, confusion, or boredom. Body language and other forms of non-verbal communication vary across cultures and between individuals so it is difficult to generalize or adopt simple formulas. However, among members of the same culture there is often some agreement about meanings as well as preferred ways to look and act in a particular situation. For example, poised American speakers do not stand absolutely still when they teach, nor do they sway from side to side, or frequently adjust their clothing. While not standing very close to any one individual student, they also do not remove themselves from contact with the class by standing in a corner or staying at the blackboard and rarely facing the class.

The best way to become aware of how you stand and move when addressing a group is to ask for reactions from a colleague or to see yourself on videotape if your university offers this service. You can also compare your interpretations of students' body language with observations of some

"I've had both good and bad foreign teaching assistants. There are problems with their accents and there are problems with cultural and language barriers. But I think all of that can be made up for by enthusiasm for the subject matter and interest in the students."
—an American student

American teachers: for example, are the students sitting forward, in a way that suggests interest or readiness to speak? Or are they shifting around restlessly, in a way that suggests boredom? After observing others, it is up to you to decide how much attention to pay to your own body language. However, you will teach more effectively if you are alert to nuances in your students' behavior, and use their clues to adjust your teaching.

Every culture has unstated rules about how close people can stand when they are talking to one another, and under what circumstances people can touch one another. In the United States, for example, you risk misunderstanding by standing too close to someone. The most prudent course is to avoid touching others. If you notice that people back away when you are talking to them, you are probably standing closer than is comfortable in this culture. If you touch Americans when you talk to them—even by putting your hand on their arm or shoulder—you may notice that they move away unless they know you very well. In teacher to student or colleague to colleague relationships, it is not the custom to touch; if a teacher touches a student, the teacher may be open to serious criticism. Touching, irrespective of your intent, can imply an insult, condescension, or sexual interest. Most Americans say "excuse me" if they touch someone by accident. Observe what others do, and ask someone if you are in doubt.

2. Voice

Your voice is essential to your teaching. Energy and life in your voice convey interest in your subject; variety in your voice helps hold the attention of your students. If you tape yourself teaching, pay attention to the sense of yourself that you convey through your voice. Get feedback from others. Your voice can project confidence or timidity, gentleness or arrogance, interest or boredom, and your students will draw conclusions about your ability as a teacher. Adjust your voice to the size of the room. The voice of a convincing teacher projects to the back of the room. However, if the room is

"If you like something, then your enthusiasm will come through and this will make students like what you are teaching even more."
—a teaching assistant from Romania

Students in a section meeting

small, a very loud voice can overpower the students. Your voice can be confident, pleasant, or encouraging. The voice of an effective teacher in this culture does not suggest condescension, harsh criticism, or sarcasm. Your students will want to feel that they are learning from a confident teacher, but not an arrogant one. Many will be grateful for a gentle teacher, but will not respect a timid one.

3. Eye contact

Every culture has unstated rules about eye contact. Many people adjust easily and naturally to these customs without much effort. Observing others will provide the best clues for you.

Use your eyes to stay in contact with your class and to communicate with each student. Look at each student for several seconds at a time. Even when you are writing on the board or reading a text aloud, look up from time to time. Establishing eye contact with your students can also help you manage classroom interactions: looking away from speakers who dominate can imply that it is time for someone else to talk; looking at quiet students can invite their participation.

In this culture, good speakers address the audience directly and do not consistently look up over the listeners' heads; nor do they look down, avoiding the listeners' eyes. "Looking someone in the eye" conveys a sense of attention or conviction. Most speakers are not aware that they break the intensity of their gaze by blinking and by looking away from the listener every few seconds. In this culture, if this does not happen, people feel stared at. Listeners usually keep their eyes fixed on the speaker. Your students will look at you most of the time (if they are interested in what you are saying), except when they look away briefly to think, to write notes, or to avoid your eyes if they do not want to be called on to speak. It is not—as in some cultures—a sign of respect to look down.

If you watch yourself and your students on tape, notice whether you look to the left and right, and at students sitting in the corners when you teach. Do you look directly at individuals when you talk? When you look at your students, try to interpret what their eyes convey: attention, interest, concentration, agreement, disagreement, hesitation, confusion, or boredom. If you look at students' eyes, they can tell you a great deal.

4. What is going on? There must be an explanation

Curiosity about cultural expectations of teachers and students will help you develop the habit of observing what people do in different situations, especially students and teachers in and out of the classroom. Ask yourself what cultural values the behavior reflects and remain open to the possibility that the meaning of behavior may be different from what you assume.

"I will never forget my very first day as a student at an American university. First of all, I found it very degrading to sit in one of those little baby desks. Then a young man, not a whole lot older than me and wearing cut-off jeans, came in. I'm not sure if he was wearing shoes or not. He sat on the big desk in the front of the room, and said, 'Hi, my name is Jeremy.' I remember thinking, 'I don't care who you are, you'd better get off that desk. The professor will be here any minute.' I had never been taught by anyone who was not wearing academic robes, so it took me a few minutes to figure out that he was the teacher."

—a faculty member from Ireland

Graduate students discussing a case

"A student came in to see me during office hours, and asked me to her dormitory for dinner—she said it was a special night when students were inviting teachers to dinner. I had never heard of such a thing, and I didn't know why she was asking me. So I said I had to check my calendar. I discussed this with a colleague in my department and he explained to me that many students invited faculty and teaching assistants to dinner on special evenings in their dormitories, so I understood that this was not unusual."

—a teaching assistant from Egypt

"When I was a freshman, a visiting professor from Lebanon returned a set of papers to the class. As he handed them back, he commented on how pleased he was that everyone did so well. However, the students looked depressed when they got their papers back. The professor must have mentioned this to someone, because at the next class he apologized. According to the grading system he was accustomed to, a score of 70% is a reason to celebrate. The American system is much more liberal with high grades."

—a faculty member from Kenya

Living and teaching in a different culture can be both maddening and fascinating. Interpreting the significance of many small events you observe or experience can be elusive. To keep life in the United States more fascinating than maddening, develop a perspective of raising questions about your observations. Sometimes if you watch and wait, the situation will become clear. At other times it will be clear that you do not understand the meaning of events. When you are in doubt or simply curious, say so. This may also give you a chance to share something about your culture. The most potentially troublesome times are when you think you understand what happened, but you have misinterpreted the significance of words, gestures, or actions. If you make a habit of watching others, noticing puzzling aspects of situations, and discussing them with your American colleagues, you will learn a great deal about the culture.

Teaching American students is not always easy for faculty and teaching assistants from other cultures, especially at the beginning. However, if you anticipate some of the differences you will encounter in the classroom—and if you are prepared with some strategies to communicate with your students—a difficult job can be made easier. You will enjoy your teaching—and your students—more.

VII   *Appendices*

The following supplements are based on resource materials at the Derek Bok Center for Teaching and Learning. Some were written by Bok Center staff for their work with different courses and programs. Others are handouts used at teaching orientation sessions conducted by faculty and teaching assistants with successful classroom experience. While many teachers have found these materials and handouts helpful, you may find the advice idiosyncratic and even contradictory. It is important to be aware of the traditions of the course you are teaching. If you are a teaching assistant, it is important to remember that the course is not your own. You may respectfully differ from the professor, but in the end you are a member of a team.

Course Preparation Questions

In preparing a syllabus, consider the following:

- **What do you want to have happen in this course?** What is your purpose in teaching the course? What do you hope to teach the students? What do you hope they will know at the end?

- **What are your students' capacities and expectations?** What is your audience? Who are your students? How much can you expect them to know already? What level of sophistication can you expect? How much can you expect them to do? What courses have they taken?

Those are the two primary questions. The other questions follow from them.

- How are you going to tie the course together? What is the story line for the course? What are the logical links between sessions? And how will you enable the students to follow the course's progression from week to week?

- How are you going to let your students know the overall plan for the course, including suggested readings, non-reading assignments, when written material will be due and what it will consist of?

- What activities other than the readings and class discussions might be appropriate?

- How are you going to get to the broader or underlying conceptual issues, as opposed to simply covering the material?

- How are you going to include material and the perspectives of previously marginalized groups, e.g., women and various minority groups?

- How flexible are you going to be to meet students' different backgrounds, interests and needs; would you be willing to change directions in the middle of the semester if that seemed appropriate? Would you be willing to entertain different approaches to the material?

- How will you get feedback from the students?

- How will you stimulate students to think about the material before class? How will you encourage or require students to prepare?

- How will you evaluate the students? How will you know where the students are in their work, what they are thinking, how well they are doing the work?

- How will you give feedback to the students?

—Prepared for leaders of small group discussions by Lee Warren, Derek Bok Center for Teaching and Learning

The First Day of Class

The first day of class makes many teachers feel nervous. Contemplating the first day stirs up their worst fears and self-doubts. But it is a very important day. The impression that students form on the first day about the teacher, as well as the course, may last the entire term. Considering the following suggestions should help a nervous first-time teacher not only to get through the first day, but also to begin establishing a good working relationship with the class. As you plan, remind yourself that you know more than you think you do, and that for many of your students the material is new.

Preparing for class

Do some research

The more you know about what to expect, the more confident you will feel. If possible, visit a lecture or section before you begin to teach, talk to someone who has taught (or taken) the course before, talk to the previous professor, or experienced teaching assistant, and look at the previous student evaluations and examinations.

- Who takes the course? Why? What is the range of their abilities?
- What are the typical problems of students and teachers?
- What are the course requirements, materials, and policies concerning such things as grading and deadlines for work?

- Who will grade the students? On what basis? What percent of the grade is the responsibility of the section leaders? The professor?
- What do students say about the course?

Visit the room ahead of time

Think about the space from the students' point of view. Will they be able to see you? Will they be able to see the board, slides, or demonstrations? If you plan to lead a discussion, will they be able to see each other (and thus be able to talk to each other)? Think about the best way to organize the space so that the layout of the room is consistent with the pedagogy. You can move chairs, plan an activity for small groups to break up a rigidly structured environment, or teach from different parts of the room. Sometimes, you can even ask for a different room if you are not satisfied with the one assigned.

Think through your plan

The more completely you have planned what you hope to accomplish the first day, the more confident you will appear. Anticipate about how much time you plan to spend on each topic. Even if they know the basic material, teaching assistants should attend lectures throughout the term and be familiar with students' reading assignments, using the same texts as the students. While most beginning teachers plan far more material than can be reasonably covered in one class, being over-prepared is more reassuring than being under-prepared.

Conducting the class

Try to view the course and the work from the students' point of view—they are interested in whether the course will meet their needs and interests, how the class will be run, how much work will be required, and how it will be graded.

In the lecture or section:

Clarify your students' expectations

The course:
- What is the course really about?
- What is the approach to the subject?
- What level of skill and comprehension does it aim for?
- What are common misconceptions?
- What is the role of the section in relation to the course?

The class:
- What kind of preparation is expected?
- Is attendance required?
- What are the policies about written work?

The work:
- How much time and effort will the course demand of the students?
- What would be your strategy if you were taking the course at their level of development and preparation?
- How will their work be graded?

In the section:

Find out something about your students

Students appreciate teachers who know their names and something about their interests. The more you know about the students in your class, the easier it will be to connect names with faces, to draw on their strengths, and to help them develop their interests.

Learn their names and use them as quickly as possible

You can begin by collecting information on index cards. For example, ask them what name they want to be called by, how to reach them, what class or program they are in (see Glossary: *Class of —*), their local address, their phone number, e-mail address, outside activities, etc. You may ask them to sign up for short visits with you in your office early in the semester. They will always know where to find you after that.

Say something about yourself

Explaining why you find your field worth studying and what you find particularly interesting will allow you to communicate your enthusiasm for the subject. Telling your students what you want to be called (and writing it on the board) will make it easier for them to talk to you.

Answer the following questions:
- Where and when do you want your students to visit or telephone you? (Give students your office hours, office location, telephone numbers, or e-mail address. Tell them what hours they may telephone.)
- What do you do besides teach this class? (e.g., If you are a graduate student, what are you studying and who is your

adviser. If you are a faculty member, what is your special interest.)

- What genuinely interests you about the subject matter of the course?

Do some actual work

Work through a specific problem or topic that illustrates what the course asks of the students and what it has to offer them. Begin to show them how you want them to participate in your class.

While some teachers devote the first day to administration and preliminary activities, most find that engaging students in actual work during the first class communicates seriousness of purpose and gives students (especially those who are shopping around) an idea of what your class will be like.

—Prepared for the *Teaching Fellows' Handbook*, Harvard University, by Ellen Sarkisian, Derek Bok Center for Teaching and Learning

Observing American Teachers and Students

One of the best ways to learn what is expected of teachers and students in another culture is to observe a class. For a range of effective teaching styles, ask a few colleagues if you can sit in on a class.

Some questions to keep in mind:

- How does this class differ from one in your own culture?
- What does the teacher do before the class formally begins? What do the students do?
- How do they interact with each other?
- How does the class formally begin?
- What is the layout of the classroom? Are the students in rows or around a table? Where is the teacher? Sitting or standing?
- What is on the board? Are there handouts?
- Does the teacher ask questions?
- Who answers them? If a student answers, how long is the answer? Do other students add to the response? What comments does the teacher make?
- Do the students ask questions about things they do not understand?
- How many students participate?
- How does the teacher find out if the students understand the content of the class?
- Look at the students' notes. What do you notice?
- Are there distinct segments of the class? How are transitions made from one topic to the next?
- How does class formally end? What does the teacher do? What do the students do?

—Prepared for the Teaching in English Program by Ellen Sarkisian, Derek Bok Center for Teaching and Learning

Office Hours

Office hours are designated as a special time when faculty and teaching assistants are available for individual consultations with students. Some teachers keep a schedule of appointments in their personal date books; some post a sign-up sheet at their office; others are available for students to drop by during a designated time block.

Two faculty members (mathematics and social science) give their ideas about the use of office hours and the comments they might make to students in that setting.

Mathematics

The mathematics professor identifies two distinct kinds of office hours: those open to all students and those for individuals seeking help.

Open office hours

Early in the term this professor gives a short ungraded quiz so that he can make sure all students are correctly placed in his course. By asking students to pick up the quiz at his office, he gives them a chance to find out where his office is and to talk one-on-one. After a series of conversations in his office, he says the interactions in his classroom change; students talk more. His basic goal is to find out that the students are in the right class.

When a student comes to his office he says something welcoming, like:

"Hey, how are you doing? Glad you dropped by."
"How was that quiz for you? Any surprises so far?"
"Does this course seem like what you were expecting so far? Why are you taking it?"
"Anything else you want to tell me about the course?"

Normally he does not ask where the student comes from or for personal information irrelevant to the course. He tries not to pry into the personal lives of his students, but may ask, "What math or science have you taken before?"

Students seeking individual help

When students come to his office because they want help, they will always have questions. However, they do not always reveal the nature of their difficulty. The conversation consists of answering questions and making sure that the students' questions are not symptoms of a bigger issue. He will ask coaxing questions about a math problem such as:

"Have you ever seen anything like this problem before? Earlier in the course? What are the ingredients? How would you begin?"
"What would the last few steps look like? How would it have to end?"

He may encourage the student to go to the board:

"Let's try it. Just write it down. What does the problem tell you?"
"Is there anything else you know that might help?"
"What is the first thing you might try?"

He may end the meeting by asking the student to summarize what they have just done, offering encouragement, and an invitation to return:

"What do you think are the main points of what we've just done?"
"Is there anything else I can help you with?"
"OK, well, keep trying. If you run into problems like this again, drop by."

If a student asking for help is in real academic trouble, the professor tries to be realistic about what the student can do. He will probably ask about study habits:

"How do you study for this course? How much time do you spend? What do you do?"
"Are there other students in the course that you talk to about this? Many students find it helpful to talk over general principles on a regular basis with others in the course. Why don't you look at the list of phone numbers?"

It is not unusual for students in trouble to cry, so he keeps a box of tissues in his office. He says this situation can make teachers feel helpless, but handing the student a box of tissues acknowledges, without words, that the teacher has noticed. When he must take further steps, he reminds the students of resources for study assistance or counseling. He may suggest they leave the course if they are misplaced. At the close of the meeting, he tries to summarize next steps and open the opportunity for follow-up:

"Look, you are going to do this, check with that person. And I will...."
"Is there anything else I can do?"
"Check with me in a week or two and let me know how it's going."

Social Science

The social science professor reflects on drop-in visits during office hours. In this case, before focusing on the work of the meeting, the conversation moves slowly at the beginning, with pauses and open questions that might reveal the reason for the visit.

Opening the meeting with a student

Because it might be difficult for students to cross the threshold of his office, psychologically or physically, he tries to invite them in:

"Hi. How are you?"
"Come on in."
"Welcome. Have a seat."

If the meeting was not scheduled, the student may ask if this is a bad time. He offers possible responses:

"This is a good time. I'm not expecting another student for 15 minutes or so."
"Could you wait just a few minutes?"

If there is a choice, the student may not know where to sit. He usually asks them to choose or to position the chair, to give the student a measure of control.

"Where would you like to sit?"
"Is this comfortable?"
"Do you want to pull a chair over to the table?"

Some students prefer privacy, others may be anxious about a closed space. He usually leaves the door ajar, but allows the student to close it. This is especially important if gender or intimacy issues might arise.

Setting a climate

To avoid seeming too clinical or patronizing, he generally does not say, "What can I do for you?" He says something light, with small talk to establish a connection ("Oh, I just saw..." referring to an event of mutual interest). After a little chat, to create an opening for the student to volunteer a way to begin the meeting, he may pause and say, "So...." If the student does not fill the opening, he will say something to help him figure out what the student needs, what concern motivated the visit:

> "So, what's going on?"
> "What's happening?"

A comment that personalizes the occasion often facilitates the meeting:

> "I noticed you were up on the reading today. Thanks."
> "Your project sounds interesting. Can you tell me about it."

Listening to the student

After letting the student speak, when he thinks he understands the presenting issue, he feels that it is important to know whether there are underlying or unexpressed concerns. He asks:

> "So where do you think I can be of help?"
> "Have we covered everything?"
> "What other concerns do you have about the project?"

Closing   The student may wait for the teacher to close the meeting. This professor tries to convey his interest in the student's project, but feels that it is useful to pause at the conclusion to let the student articulate a remedy or a plan of action:

> "We must wrap up in a few minutes. I'm expecting another student.
> "You have a very interesting project. So, now you plan to..."

By listening carefully and permitting the student to clarify the issues, this professor feels that he is most likely to offer the most appropriate suggestions. At the end, he may stand or, on rare occasions, offer to shake hands to conclude the visit:

> "Good luck. And, if you want to check back with me give a call."

—Based on reflections about office hours by Terry Aladjem, Social Studies and Derek Bok Center for Teaching and Learning; and Daniel Goroff, Mathematics and Derek Bok Center for Teaching and Learning.

A Checklist for Giving Lectures

Many excellent teachers teach small classes with ease, but are anxious about lecturing to large groups. If you are anxious, you are not alone. Some non-native English speakers find lecturing easier than leading discussions because they can plan ahead and control the direction of the class. One disadvantage of lecturing is that it is difficult to find out how well the students understand the class. Here are some tips from experienced lecturers on planning and delivering lectures, as well as on getting feedback from students.

Preparation

- Know your audience and prepare your talk for their level.
- Design your lecture around a theme: tell students the big picture, where the topic fits into the field, how it links with the previous lecture or the course.
- Follow the commonly quoted advice on structure: say what you are going to say; say it; say what you said. That is, provide an overview and conclusions.
- Plan the timing of your talk and estimate the mid-point. Label parts to omit if you are pressed for time.
- Check the room. Become familiar with the physical surroundings: table or lectern, lights and equipment.

Delivery

- Engage your audience. Pause from time to time. Look at different individuals in different parts of the room (front, sides, corners, back).
- Show enthusiasm for your subject. Set aside your notes to tell stories that interest you or discoveries emerging in the field.

- Express your points in a variety of ways; students have different learning styles. Use pictures, diagrams, analogies, examples, and narrative detail.
- Help your audience listen. Shift the focus of attention or style of delivery after about 20 or 30 minutes.
- End on time.

Feedback

- Invite questions at the end. Repeat the questions. When you respond, address everyone, not just the questioner.
- Alternatively, ask students to take a few minutes at the end to write questions that you can answer later, or that can be discussed in section.
- Experiment by lecturing more interactively, either taking questions from students or asking students questions during the lecture.

A final word

- The fundamental question to keep in mind: Why are you lecturing? Students can learn on their own by reading a book, so what does the lecture contribute? Answering this question in your own way will help you to plan and deliver a more effective lecture.

—Prepared for the Teaching in English Program by Ellen Sarkisian, Derek Bok Center for Teaching and Learning

Suggested Assignments for Discussion Sections

The purpose of a discussion is to give students a chance to express their understanding of the reading, to formulate their own ideas and questions, and to stimulate one another's thinking. You can guide their understanding by giving assignments to prepare and you can stimulate their thinking by the way you organize the discussion.

Before Class

- The instructor assigns a carefully selected passage or sub-section from the week's reading and hands out a small number of study questions in advance of the section meeting.
- Each student prepares, in writing, three questions about the assigned material.
- Each student collects, and lists in writing, several related instances, examples, or quotations from the assigned material.
- Each student prepares a one- or two-page written response to the assigned material or to the week's lectures.
- Each student summarizes, in writing, the main idea presented in one of the week's lectures.
- Each student prepares, in writing, one or two statements that might be regarded as basic truths, straightforward facts, or essential presuppositions on which more complex discussions can build.
- The instructor divides students into groups of two or three to prepare ahead of time for the section meeting. Each group chooses a spokesperson and prepares brief written headings or questions.

- The instructor pairs the assigned material with an example from a different historical period or a different sociological or cultural setting. The emphasis should be on the unexpected juxtaposition: the example chosen should be compact and manageable.

In Class
- Students as a group brainstorm in the classroom about a question or issue raised by the teacher. Write all the ideas on the board before organizing or discussing them.
- Each student writes a one-minute in-class response to a question or statement from the teacher. This exercise is followed by a class discussion.

—Prepared for a Derek Bok Center Teaching Orientation by Judith Ryan, German and Comparative Literature

Some Issues in Science Section Teaching

Appropriate vs. Inappropriate Activities

Appropriate
- Providing practice and feedback in problem-solving
- Presenting problem-solving strategies
- Following up on issues raised in lecture
- Summarizing
- Showing how a scientist approaches a problem
- Relating the subject to your own experience
- Asking and answering questions
- Giving students practice working at the board

Inappropriate
- Repeating last lecture
- Delivering next lecture
- Introducing new notation or mathematical formalism
- Working problem set for the class
- Spending the whole hour answering the first question
- Facing the board (ignoring the students)
- Teaching to top or bottom group of students
- Putting students down
- Undermining the professor, the course, or the text

Organization vs. flexibility

Argument for organization: material has logical order so it is best to follow that order

Argument for flexibility: you can't know what students will want to talk about and it is best to respond to their needs

Compromise: ask for problem areas at beginning then order the discussion as you think best

Reacting to what happens in lecture

In the professor's lecture the teaching assistant can learn:
- Professor's ideas of what is important
- Order in which material is presented
- What has been presented clearly and what hasn't
- Concepts that need examples
- What's taken for granted
- Teacher's notation
- Level of math
- Loose ends that need to be tied up

Strategies for encouraging participation

- Present a problem; go down a row of students and ask everyone to make some contribution toward solving the problem.
- Present a problem and take a vote on the correct solution or next step.
- Work an example with many 2- or 3-way choices; ask for votes on each.
- Give different problems to groups of 2-3 students, then have someone from each group present the problem at the board.
- Start everyone working on a problem; wander around answering questions; a few of the first students to finish put different parts of the solution on board while others continue working; students then present parts of the solution and lead discussion.
- Have students give short presentations on prepared topics.

Tips on blackboard technique

- Try to visualize the finished board before you start to write.
- Find out where the chalk is stored.
- Make board layout reflect the organization of what you are discussing.
- Spell out technical terms on the board, especially new ones.
- Don't stand in front of what you just wrote.
- Read aloud what you write as you write it.
- When changing topics, stop, ask for questions, and then erase the entire board.
- See what your students' notes look like. Much of what you write but little of what you say will probably be there.

—Developed by science teaching assistants in a Derek Bok Center Teaching Orientation session led by Jed Dempsey, Physics

Teaching Tips for Science Section Leaders

- Put an outline on the board at the beginning of class. Try to follow it.
- Clearly state the big picture: Where does today's section fit into the course? How does it follow last week's section? What is coming up next week?
- Get to know your students. Let them get to know you.
- Go outside and take a class picture after the first section. Use it to learn names.
- Call students by name. Include them in examples.
- Look at your students when they are responding to you; don't use it as time to glance down at your notes. It is impolite not to give your full attention when someone is speaking.
- Don't interrupt...and give students a long time to think before expecting a response to your questions. It isn't easy for students to think on their feet, especially if they are shy.
- Loudly proclaim: "this is a take-home message" (approximately three times per section)
- Before section (or after), ask students to tell you about their best section. Ask them about their worst section and why it wasn't very good. Students have a lot to say about what is useful and what is not. They have especially strong thoughts about how section shouldn't be taught.
- How NOT to have an interactive section: by asking very simple questions. It is patronizing. No one wants to answer a clearly easy question. Ask genuine questions that demand thoughtful answers.
- Don't teach lists of facts: why waste section time on something that can be memorized? When things must be memorized, make a summary handout.

- Ask to see a student's notes sometime (after class is over). Notice that everything you wrote on the board is in the notes verbatim. What isn't written on the board will be a bit more sketchy in the notes. If you want information in students' notes, write it on the board.
- NEVER go over your allotted time. EVER.

Take-home message #1:   When you don't allow simple, passive attendance in section, you get active, engaged minds.

Take-home message #2:   Students who re-invent the wheel in section will understand it better than if you just hand them a wheel when they walk in.

Take-home message #3:   If there is one thing a student doesn't want to be forced to do, it is to answer a really obvious question, a clearly easy question. Ask genuine questions that demand thoughtful answers.

—Prepared for a Derek Bok Center Teaching Orientation by Jay Phelan, Biology

Grading Problem Sets

Make sure the general grading criteria and procedures are clear from the beginning. The standard for grading is set by the professor. If a particular single answer is acceptable, that is what to look for. If the professor says that grading is up to the teaching assistants, they must resolve the following issues and communicate their expectations to their students.

- Announce the policy about working together. It's best to put the policy in writing.
- Announce the policy about late assignments and other excuses.
- Some courses allow or encourage students to revise problem sets and hand them in again. Will you accept these? Give credit?
- Insist on clear expression and style. Give examples in writing and in class.
- Students often appreciate comments and encouragement, not just numerical scores.
- Too many students approach problem sets mechanically. Try to make sure they really understand.
- If students are thinking about the process and using information correctly, will you give them partial credit even if the answer is wrong?
- If students write a great deal, mention the correct answer, but include other sentences that show they don't understand, will you give credit for the right answer?
- What if the formulas are correct, but a calculation is wrong?
- Be aware that what may seem to be minor computational errors can mask serious conceptual errors.

- Students learn more if you can indicate the source of an error rather than just marking it incorrect.
- Share papers and grades with colleagues to see if you are scoring too high or too low.

A study group works together on a problem set

—Prepared by Mike Dyer, Biology, and Daniel Goroff, Derek Bok Center for Teaching and Learning

Writing Laboratory Reports

A Note to the Lab Instructor

Laboratory reports can be among the most challenging and rewarding aspects of a laboratory section for both instructors and students. Students write better lab reports when you set high expectations and offer strategies to meet them.

A Note about Grammar, Spelling, and Style

Set aside a significant portion of the grade, for example 25%, for grammar, spelling, and style. Some lab instructors find the following strategy helpful:

If the content of the lab report is excellent but poorly written, students lose a predetermined number of points (25%) rather than a point here or there for run-on sentences or misspelled words. Because this grading policy is demanding, students can be given an option to improve their writing. They can exchange rough drafts of their lab reports with a partner and edit the drafts. Then they can make changes and turn in a copy of the final draft, along with the rough draft and comments. If students make a genuine effort to edit their partners' lab reports and respond to their partners' comments, then they receive full credit for the portion of the grade set aside for grammar, spelling and style. Most students choose this option; as a result, the quality of their writing usually improves dramatically.

A Note about References

Students should be shown sample lab reports or journal articles that use the style preferred in the course. Or they may be referred to a standard guide such as *A Manual for Writers* by Kate Turabian.

Strategies

- Clearly outline your expectations in writing.
- Tell students which aspects of the experiment to focus on.
- Challenge students to express some of their own ideas on the experimental results, especially the results that relate to other aspects of the course.
- Encourage students to form study groups, look up references in the library, and come to office hours.

Here is an outline to help you set expectations on laboratory reports. Your emphasis may be different. Your own handouts to students should include details that are relevant to a particular assignment.

Laboratory Report Guide for Students

Title

The title is a descriptive statement that tells the reader what experimental system you are using and the most important result. The title should be complete and informative.

Example

Revival and Identification of Bacterial Spores in 25- to 40-Million-Year-Old Dominican Amber

[*Science* (268) 1060-1064. Examples in the sections that follow are adapted from this article.]

Abstract

The abstract is a concise statement of the problem and conclusions of the experiment. The abstract helps readers decide if they want to read the rest of the paper. While readers may look at the abstract first when browsing a journal, researchers usually write the abstract last.

Answer the following questions, for a total of four or five sentences:

- What system did you study?

  ...bacterial spores from the abdominal content of an extinct bee species found in Dominican amber...

- What process did you use?

  ...decontaminated the surface of the amber and used aseptic procedures to recover and culture the bacterium...

- What were your results?

> ...bacterium that was isolated is an ancient species related to *Bacillus sphaericus*, not an extant contaminant...

- What are the implications of this discovery?

> ...implications for evolutionary biology...

Introduction

The introduction should convince readers who are unfamiliar with the experimental system that the system is appropriate to answer the problem described in the abstract. Readers who are familiar with the field often skip the introduction.

The following should be included in the introduction, for a total of four to six paragraphs:

- Describe where the problem you are studying fits in the context of the general field.

> A fundamental goal of evolutionary biology is to construct phylogenetic trees based on DNA sequence homology and to derive an accurate nucleotide substitution rate.

> It is useful to have DNA isolates from ancient sources such as preserved bones, insects and bacteria.

> The problem is establishing that the DNA is ancient and not a contaminant. In many cases there is very little DNA and the amount of DNA sequence data that can be obtained is limited.

- Describe why your system is well-suited to answer the question.

> Ancient bacterial spores such as *Bacillus* are an excellent source of primitive DNA for evolutionary studies. The DNA remains virtually intact over millions of years and in some cases the bacteria can be revived and cultured, providing an endless source of DNA for sequence analysis.

- Describe the system being studied.

> Bees and *Bacillus*, both modern and ancient, have symbiotic relationships.

> Amber is a good source of ancient bees.

- Describe the details of the experimental system and restate your findings in the last sentence.

We isolated an ancient *Bacillus* from the contents of the abdomen of a bee preserved in Dominican amber and derived some DNA sequence data which will be useful for evolutionary studies....

Materials and Methods

Each experimental procedure should be described in a separate section, usually one paragraph.

Sample section titles:

Isolation and decontamination of the amber
Aseptic procedures used to isolate the *Bacillus* spores from the amber
Growth of *Bacillus*
Characterization of *Bacillus*

Results

The results should be presented in a logical order to make the conclusions clear for the reader. They do not have to be presented in the order in which the experiments were performed. Arguments or opinions should not be presented in this section; those should be saved for the discussion. The length of the results section will depend on the particular system being studied and the experiments that were performed, but 4-6 paragraphs is usually a reasonable goal.

• What is the source of the sample being studied?

...fossil bees in 25-40-million-year-old Dominican amber.

• What preparation or initial characterization of the sample did you perform?

The amber was surface-sterilized, cracked, and the abdominal contents of the fossil bee were harvested in a sterile hood.

Spores were grown in trypticase soy broth at 35°C.

• What experiments did you perform on the sample?

...the spores that we isolated and cultured were related to *Bacillus sphaericus*.

...the 16s rDNA was sequenced and we constructed a phylogenetic tree [include figure]...

...a nucleotide substitution rate was calculated and is 2×10^{-9} nucleotides per site per year...

- What control experiments did you perform?

  > ...surface-sterilization was shown to be effective by inoculating pieces of amber in media...

  > ...controls for DNA isolation and amplification showed that there were no contaminations...

  > ...the room that we used for these experiments was used only for ancient isolates...

A Note about the Figures
Make sure the students understand what the figures should look like, what tables or charts need to be included and what calculations need to be performed. Make sure students know when to connect data points on a graph and when to give a best-fit approximation. Ask students to label all axes clearly, to give the figures descriptive titles, and to provide a figure legend.

Discussion

Conclusions should be presented in the discussion section. If the results are presented in a logical order, the reader should come to the same conclusions as the author. Include the following in the discussion section, one paragraph for each element:

- Retrace the logic of your results and how that led to your conclusions.

  > ...a 25-40 million-year-old isolate of *Bacillus sphaericus* was cultured...

  > ...the DNA was sequenced and we constructed a phylogenetic tree...

  > ...we calculated a nucleotide substitution rate...

  > ...all of our evidence suggests that this isolate is truly an ancient bacterium...

- Are there other possible conclusions? Does your work agree with the work of others?

  > ...it is still possible that the bacteria we characterized is not truly ancient but an extant contaminant...

...this is unlikely because we performed the appropriate control experiments...

...our calculation of nucleotide substitution rate is different from previous calculations by others and we believe this discrepancy may be due to...

- How do the results advance your field? What experiments should be done next? Are there broader implications of your work?

   ...we have advanced the field by describing a method for isolating ancient bacterial spores free of contamination...

   ...we are now working on analyzing more isolates and sequencing more DNA to resolve the difference between our nucleotide substitution rate and that calculated by others...

   ...such ancient isolates will help evolutionary biologists construct phylogenetic trees and come to an agreed upon nucleotide substitution rate which can be used in other experimental systems...

References   The source, the author's name, and date of publication must be indicated whenever someone else's work or ideas are discussed, paraphrased, or quoted. Names and dates may be included parenthetically in the body of the paper or numbered footnotes may be used, with references listed at the end.

—Prepared by Mike Dyer, Biology

Writing Comments About Student Papers

What is the purpose of writing comments on a student's paper?

- To explain, clarify, or justify a grade
- To indicate how the paper fulfills, or fails to fulfill, the assignment
- To help the student understand what works and what doesn't work
- To motivate the student to improve this paper or the next one
- More broadly, to help the student become a better writer

Comments in the margins or on the student's pages

Use marginal comments to address specific issues. You might offer praise. You might ask a question. You might indicate what's missing. Try to keep your comments brief. Avoid overwhelming the student. Sample comments:

> "Good point."
> "Interesting."
> "Yes."
> "✓" (indicates a point well made)
> "What do you mean here?"
> "I don't understand what you mean here."
> "Can you make this point clearer?"
> "Can you be more explicit?"
> "What is your evidence?"
> "How can you back this up?"
> "Example?"
> "Can you make this point more directly?"
> "This statement...doesn't belong here."

Comments at the end

Use end comments to provide an overview of the paper's strengths and weaknesses. Writing them on a separate page is preferable because it allows you to re-evaluate the grade or comments after you have a sense of all the students' papers.

Look for things to praise   Start with a positive comment. If the paper goes beyond the requirements, tell the student why it is outstanding. Sample comments:

> "You have gone beyond the requirements by..."
> "This paper has a good strong introduction. It tells me what the paper will be about..." (You could briefly recapitulate the argument.)
> "I like what you say about..."
> "You introduce your subject well."
> "You understand what **X** says about..."
> "You argue here that..."

In dealing with problems, be precise. Concentrate on two or three issues. Select examples from the paper. Ask questions that will stimulate responses. Sample comments:

> "Your opening repeats the instructions but it doesn't tell me what the paper is going to be about."
> "Your analysis of **X** is not clear to me." (You can also tell the student why.)
> "I find a contradiction in your discussion of..."
> "You start out talking about **X** and you end up talking about **y**."
> "To support this argument, you could have..."
> "You have summarized the reading [lecture] here, but you haven't told me what is important about it or explained why it matters."
> "You summarize **x**, but you haven't taken a position of your own."
> "On page **x**, you say ...What's the connection between this claim and the one above it [the statements that follow]?"
> "I'm not convinced that you understand what **X** means by ..." (You could also be more explicit and tell the student what **X** means.)
> "I find your argument hard to follow because..."
> "You have not covered the issue of..."

Grammar and Spelling   If the paper has many errors in grammar and spelling, avoid line-editing the whole paper. Choose a sample paragraph or two to demonstrate typical errors to the student.

Major Problems   If the paper has major problems, or problems that you cannot easily define, ask the student to see you after class or in a short conference. If you suspect plagiarism or a misuse of sources, consult with someone in authority and refer to your institution's published policies and procedures.

—Prepared for the Graduate Writing Fellows Program by Sue Lonoff, Derek Bok Center for Teaching and Learning

Grading Papers

The following remarks are intended to give you a sense of criteria for grading papers. Note that four topics recur: thesis, use of evidence, design (organization), and basic writing skills (grammar, mechanics, spelling).

The Unsatisfactory Paper

The D or F paper either has no thesis or else it has one that is strikingly vague, broad, or uninteresting. There is little indication that the writer understands the material being presented. The paragraphs do not hold together; ideas do not develop from sentence to sentence. This paper usually repeats the same thoughts again and again, perhaps in slightly different language but often in the same words. The D or F paper is filled with mechanical faults, errors in grammar, and errors in spelling.

The C Paper

The C paper has a thesis, but it is vague and broad, or else it is uninteresting or obvious. It does not advance an argument that anyone might care to debate. "Henry James wrote some interesting novels." "Modern cities are interesting places."

The thesis in a C paper often hangs on some personal opinion. If the writer is a recognized authority, such an expression of personal taste may be noteworthy, but writers gain authority not merely by expressing their tastes but by justifying them. Personal opinion is often the engine that drives an argument, but opinion by itself is never sufficient. It must be defended.

The C paper rarely uses evidence well; sometimes it does not use evidence at all. Even if it has a clear and interesting thesis, a paper with insufficient supporting evidence is a C paper. The C paper often has mechanical faults, errors in grammar and spelling, but please note: a paper without such flaws may still be a C paper.

The B Paper

The reader of a B paper knows exactly what the author wants to say. It is well organized, it presents a worthwhile and interesting idea, and the idea is supported by sound evidence presented in a neat and orderly way. Some of the sentences may not be elegant, but they are clear, and in them thought follows naturally on thought. The paragraphs may be unwieldy now and then, but they are organized around one main idea. The reader does not have to read a paragraph two or three times to get the thought that the writer is trying to convey.

The B paper is always mechanically correct. The spelling is good, and the punctuation is accurate. Above all, the paper makes sense throughout. It has a thesis that is limited and worth arguing. It does not contain unexpected digressions, and it ends by keeping the promise to argue and inform that the writer makes in the beginning.

The A Paper

The A paper has all the good qualities of the B paper, but in addition it is lively, well paced, interesting, even exciting. The paper has style. Everything in it seems to fit the thesis exactly. It may have a proofreading error or two, or even a misspelled word, but the reader feels that these errors are the consequence of the normal accidents all good writers encounter.

Reading the paper, we can feel a mind at work. We are convinced that the writer cares for his or her ideas, and about the language that carries them.

The sure mark of an A paper is that you will find yourself telling someone else about it.

—Prepared by Lewis Hyde, based on Richard Marius's guidelines for Expository Writing; edited for distribution in undergraduate courses by Sue Lonoff, Derek Bok Center for Teaching and Learning

What is Sexual Harassment?

Legal definition

Sexual harassment is a form of sex discrimination, illegal under Title VII of the 1964 Civil Rights Act. The American Medical Association has adapted Title VII guidelines to provide guidance for students, faculty, and employees.

Unwelcome sexual advances, requests for sexual favors, and other verbal or physical conduct of a sexual nature constitute sexual harassment when:

(1) submission to such conduct is made either explicitly or implicitly a term or condition of an individual's employment or academic success
(2) submission to or rejection of such conduct by an individual is used as the basis for employment or academic decisions affecting such individuals
(3) such conduct has the purpose or effect of unreasonably interfering with an individual's work or academic performance or creating an intimidating, hostile, or offensive working environment

Examples of sexual harassment may include unwelcome sexual advances that are physical, such as the 'unnecessary' touching of someone's body, or verbal, such as repeated 'sexist' jokes or slurs. Other examples include suggestions about exchanges of sexual favors which are not desired by the other party, linked to rewards related to school or work. Both men and women can be sexual harassers.

If you have authority over students

Consider your own conduct. You are expected to behave responsibly. If you evaluate the performance of students or influence a person's professional future, be careful not to misuse the power that has been entrusted to you.

- *'No'* means *'No.'* Do not repeat behavior you have been told is unwelcome. For example, unwanted persistent requests for dates or repeated remarks or physical overtures of a sexual nature can be illegal.
- *Do not interpret someone's silence as consent.*
- *In general, if you treat every person with respect and dignity* you are less likely to be misunderstood.

If you think you are being sexually harassed

Sexual harassment is always inappropriate. Any gesture or remark of a sexual nature that makes you feel uncomfortable or pressured may be a sign that you are experiencing sexual harassment. If you are harassed, do not blame yourself. Do not remain silent. Act quickly.

- Say *'No.'* Tell the person that his or her behavior toward you is making you uncomfortable.
- *Tell someone*, a friend, a colleague, or your supervisor.
- *Request an intervention from a third party.*
- *Keep a record* of events, with dates and witnesses.
- *Document your work* and evaluations so that you can attest to the quality of your performance if the accused harasser questions your abilities.
- *File a formal grievance.*

If you are a peer or colleague

Verbal or physical actions between peers or colleagues may be interpreted as sexual harassment if those actions are not asked for, not welcomed or not returned.

- *Be aware* that sexual remarks or physical conduct of a sexual nature can make some people uncomfortable even if you wouldn't feel this way yourself. People are different. Respect those differences.
- *Do not repeat behavior if you have been told it is unwanted.*
- *Do not take the risk* of discovering that your behavior is objectionable to another. If you are in doubt, stop the behavior.

—Adapted from the pamphlet *About Sexual Harassment* developed by the Ombuds Office of the Harvard Medical Area. Similar publications are available at most institutions.

Glossary

Class of —

Students identify themselves as belonging to the "class" of a particular year, referring to the date of their anticipated graduation from college. Students who began college in the fall of 2000 belong to the Class of 2004, usually expressed as '04.

concentration

The field of study an undergraduate chooses to specialize in. (At most colleges, students choose a "major.")

core

A core course or a core curriculum refers to a course or set of courses that all students must take.

course evaluations

In many colleges and universities students write an evaluation of the course. These evaluations are usually sent to the instructor, and they are often published for other students to read.

course head

The faculty member responsible for the teaching of a course.

curriculum

The goals, objectives, and sequence of activities in a course of study.

elective

A course that a student chooses (that is, a course which is not required).

freshmen

First-year college students (also called "first-years").

head teaching assistant	Most large courses have a head teaching assistant (usually a teaching assistant with previous experience in the course) who works with the course head to help organize the course and to help the other teaching assistants.
junior	A student in the third year of college.
major	The field of study an undergraduate chooses to specialize in.
office hours	Each faculty member and teaching assistant designates office hours, or special times set aside for meeting with their students. Some prefer their students to make appointments; others are available for students to drop by their office.
plagiarism	To copy ideas or words from another source and pass them on as one's own.
reading period	Several days are set aside at the end of the semester for students to do further reading in their courses after their classes are over and before exams begin.
SAT	Standardized tests of verbal and mathematical reasoning ability (Scholastic Aptitude Tests) as well as achievement tests are given at many locations across the country at certain times throughout the year by a private organization. Many colleges require high school students to submit their scores on these tests with their college applications.
section	Sections are small classes in which students have a chance to participate in discussions and ask questions. Sections may also be called recitations, labs, problem sessions, or discussion classes. Weekly section meetings, usually led by a teaching assistant, supplement the lectures in a course.
senior	A student in the fourth (and last) year of college.

shopping	In some universities at the beginning of each semester, students need not decide which courses to take until after the first week of classes. Sometimes, students may change courses a few weeks after the semester has begun. Instructors and section leaders may not be sure who is in their class until the first assignment is due.
small talk	The conversations that typically follow "Hello, how are you?" on subjects such as the surroundings ("I wonder when they will ever finish that construction?") or current topics of common interest ("That was an interesting lecture today, wasn't it?"). The art of making conversation apart from seriously pursuing specific topics or getting business accomplished consists of finding common interests and chatting about them.
sophomore	A student in the second year of college.
syllabus	A course outline that usually includes the goals of the course, dates that different topics will be covered, dates of assignments and exams. Usually the name, office address, telephone number, and e-mail address of the professor are listed at the beginning and a reading list or bibliography is at the end.
teaching assistant	Teaching assistants work under the supervision of a faculty member who is responsible for the course. Their duties may include finding and preparing course materials, teaching sections or labs, conducting tutorials, recommending grades, supervising independent study projects, and monitoring students' progress. The duties vary from course to course. In some large courses, teaching assistants may participate as a team with the course head, and they may share responsibility for writing and grading examination questions, problem sets, and papers.
tutorial	Individual or small group instruction in the student's major.
upper-classman	A student in the second (sophomore), third (junior), or last (senior) year of college.

Resources for Faculty and Teaching Assistants

Dean of Students. Administrator responsible for the well-being of students and the quality of student life.

English as a Second Language. Classes in English for non-native English speaking teaching assistants are offered at many institutions.

Health Services. Medical staff and counselors offer help for physical and emotional difficulties.

Language Laboratory. Language laboratories typically make audio tapes, video tapes, recordings or foreign short-wave radio broadcasts, and computer-aided instruction available to students and faculty.

Peer-counseling. Peer-counseling can be found for those in need of support for many of the following: academic and social issues of disabled students, contraceptives, sexual orientation, eating disorders, sexual harassment, molestation or rape, life-threatening illness or death.

Study Skills and Counseling. Many colleges and universities provide academic and personal counseling to students. Students are usually offered counseling on strategies and approaches to studying, pressures, and tension that arise from personal relations, or whatever they find affects their ability to work effectively. Some institutions offer tutoring in different subject areas, including writing. It is normally not considered appropriate for teaching assistants to tutor their own students.

Teaching Center. Advice on teaching and opportunities to improve teaching skills are offered by many institutions in a variety of formats, including workshops and individual consultations.

Work Placement or Career Counseling. Services typically include counseling, career planning, job hunting, and interview strategies.

Selected Readings On Teaching And Culture

Teaching and the Culture of the American Classroom

Althen, Gary, ed. *Learning Across Cultures*. NAFSA: Association of International Educators, 1994.

Briggs, Sarah, Victoria Clark, Carolyn Madden, Rebecca Beal, Sunny Hyon, Patricia Aldridge, and John Swales. *The International Teaching Assistant: An Annotated Critical Bibliography.* Ann Arbor: The University of Michigan, second edition, 1997.

Byrd, Patricia, Janet C. Constantinides, and Martha C. Pennington. *The Foreign Teaching Assistant's Manual*. New York: Collier Macmillan, 1989.

Plakans, Barbara. "Undergraduates' Experiences with and Attitudes towards International Teaching Assistants." In *TESOL Quarterly.* Vol. 31, no. 1 (1997): 95-119.

Smith, Jan, Colleen M. Meyers, and Amy J. Burkhalter. *Communicate: Strategies for International Teaching Assistants.* Englewood Cliffs, New Jersey: Regents/Prentice Hall, 1992.

Teaching

Brinkley, Alan, Betty Dessants, Michael Flamm, Cynthia Fleming, Charles Forcey, and Eric Rothschild. *The Chicago Handbook for Teachers: A Practical Guide to the College Classroom.* Chicago, Illinois: University of Chicago Press, 1999.

Christensen, C. Roland, David A. Garvin, and Ann Sweet, eds. *Education for Judgment: The Artistry of Discussion Leadership.* Boston, Massachusetts: Harvard Business School, 1992.

Davis, Barbara Gross. *Tools for Teaching.* San Francisco, California: Jossey-Bass, 1993.

Feldman, Kenneth A., and Michael B. Paulsen, eds. *Teaching and Learning in the College Classroom.* Needham Heights, Massachusetts: Simon and Schuster Custom Publishing, 1998.

Gullette, Margaret M., ed. *The Art and Craft of Teaching.* Cambridge, Massachusetts: Harvard University Press, 1984.

Lipson, Abigail. *The Four-Point Approach to Problem Solving in Math and Science.* Bureau of Study Counsel. Cambridge, Massachusetts: President and Fellows of Harvard University, 1994.

McKeachie, Wilbert J. *McKeachie's Teaching Tips: Strategies, Research, and Theory for College and University Teachers.* Boston, Massachusetts: Houghton Mifflin Co., tenth edition, 1999.

Menges, Robert, and Maryellen Weimar, eds. *Teaching on Solid Ground: Using Scholarship to Improve Practice.* San Francisco, California: Jossey-Bass, 1995.

Nelson, G. L. "Effective Teaching Behavior for International Teaching Assistants." In *Preparing the Professoriate of Tomorrow to Teach: Selected Readings in TA Training.* J. D. Nyquist, R. D. Abbott, D. H. Wulff, and J. Sprague, eds. Dubuque, Iowa: Kendall/Hunt, 1991.

Rosenthal, Robert. "How Students Learn, Part II." In *On Teaching and Learning,* vol. 3, Cambridge, Massachusetts: Harvard-Danforth Center for Teaching and Learning, 1989.

Sarkisian, Ellen. *Working in Groups.* Cambridge, Massachusetts: Derek Bok Center for Teaching and Learning, 1994.

Smith, R. M., P. Byrd, G. L. Nelson, R. P. Barrett, and J. C. Constantinides. *Crossing Pedagogical Oceans: International Teaching Assistants in U.S. Undergraduate Education.* ASHE-ERIC Higher Education Report No. 8. Washington, D.C.: The George Washington University, School of Education and Human Development, 1992.

Teaching Fellows Handbook. Cambridge, Massachusetts: Harvard Graduate School of Arts and Sciences, 2000.

"Tips for Teachers: Sensitivity to Women in the Contemporary Classroom." Cambridge, Massachusetts: Derek Bok Center for Teaching and Learning, 1994.

"Tips for Teachers: Twenty Ways to Make Lectures More Participatory." Cambridge, Massachusetts: Derek Bok Center for Teaching and Learning, 1994.

Weimar, Maryellen, and Rose Ann Neff. *Teaching College: Collected Readings for the New Instructor.* Madison, Wisconsin: Atwood Publishing, 1998.

Winkelmes, Mary-Ann, and James Wilkinson, eds. *Voices of Experience: Observations from a Harvard Teaching Seminar.* New York: Peter Lang, Inc., forthcoming.

Culture

Gochenour, Theodore, ed. *Beyond Experience: The Existential Approach to Cross-Cultural Education.* Yarmouth, Maine: Intercultural Press, Inc., second edition, 1993.

Hall, Edward T. *The Silent Language.* New York: Anchor Doubleday Books, 1990.

Intercultural Press, Inc., P.O. Box 700, Yarmouth, Maine, 04096. List of publications. Website: www.interculturalpress.com

Kauffmann, Norman L., Judith N. Martin, and Henry D. Weaver, with Judy Weaver. *Students Abroad: Strangers at Home.* Yarmouth, Maine: Intercultural Press, Inc., 1992.

Lanier, Alison. Revised by C. William Gay. *Living in the U.S.A.* Yarmouth, Maine: Intercultural Press, Inc., 5th edition, 1996.

Levine, Dena, and Mara Adelman. *Beyond Language: Cross-Cultural Communication.* Englewood Cliffs, New Jersey: Prentice Hall, 1992.

National Association for Foreign Student Affairs. 1307 New York Avenue, NW, Eighth Floor, Washington, D.C., 20005-4701. Annual list of publications. Website: www.nafsa.org/

Paige, R. Michael, ed. *Education for the Intercultural Experience.* Yarmouth, Maine: Intercultural Press, Inc., 1993.

Stewart, Edward C., and Milton J. Bennett. *American Cultural Patterns: A Cross-Cultural Perspective.* Yarmouth, Maine: Intercultural Press, Inc., 1991.

Storti, Craig. *Cross-Cultural Dialogues: 74 Brief Encounters with Cultural Difference.* Yarmouth, Maine: Intercultural Press, Inc. 1994.

Selected Readings On Teacher Training

Bailey, Kathleen M., Frank Pialorsi, and Jean Zukowski/Faust, eds. *Foreign Teaching Assistants in U. S. Universities.* Washington, D.C.: National Association for Foreign Student Affairs, 1984.

Barnes, Louis B., C. Roland Christensen, and Abby J. Hansen. *Teaching and the Case Method.* Boston: Harvard Business School, 1994.

Bauer, Gabriele, and Mark Tanner, eds. *Current Approaches to International TA Preparation in Higher Education: A Collection of Program Descriptions.* Seattle: Center for Instructional Development, University of Washington, 1994.

Case, Bettye Anne, ed. *You're the Professor, What Next? Ideas and Resources for Preparing College Teachers.* MAA Notes, Number 35. Washington, D.C.: Mathematical Association of America, 1994.

Katz, Joseph, and Mildred Henry. *Turning Professors into Teachers: A New Approach to Faculty Development and Student Learning.* New York: MacMillan, 1988.

Madden, Carolyn G., and Cynthia L. Myers, eds. *Discourse and Performance of International Teaching Assistants.* Alexandria, Virginia: TESOL, 1994.

Marincovich, Michele, Jack Prostko, and Frederic Stout, eds. *The Professional Development of Graduate Teaching Assistants.* Bolton, Massachusetts: Anker Publishing Company, Inc., 1998.

Nyquist, Jody D., Robert D. Abbott, Donald H. Wulff, and Jo Sprague, eds. *Preparing the Professoriate of Tomorrow to*

Teach: Selected Readings in TA Training. Dubuque, Iowa: Kendall/Hunt Publishing Company, 1991.

Ramsden, Paul. *Learning to Teach in Higher Education.* London: Routledge, 1992.

Samovar, Larry A., and Richard E. Porter, eds. *Intercultural Communication: A Reader.* Belmont, California: Wadsworth Publishing Co., ninth edition, 1999.

Steen, Lynn Arthur. *Heading the Call for Change: Suggestions for Curricular Action.* Washington, D.C.: Mathematical Association of America, 1992.

Tobias, Sheila. *They're Not Dumb, They're Different: Stalking the Second Tier.* Tucson, Arizona: Research Corporation, 1994.

Travers, Paul D. "Better Training for Teaching Assistants." In *College Teaching*. Vol. 37, no. 4 (1989): 147-149.

Weston C., and P.A. Cranton. "Selecting Instructional Strategies." In *The Journal of Higher Education*. Vol. 57, no. 3 (May/June 1986): 259-88.

Selected Books And Tapes On Speaking, Listening, And Usage

Boyd, Frances, David Quinn, and Garrison Keillor. *Stories from Lake Wobegon: Advanced Listening and Conversation Skills.* New York: Longman, 1990. (book and audiotape)

Burke, David. *Street Talk -1-: How to Speak and Understand American Slang.* Los Angeles: Optima Books, 1992. (book and audiotape)

Chwat, Sam. *Speak Up! Asian, Indian, and Middle Eastern Accent Elimination Program.* New York: Crown Publishers, Inc., 1994. (book and audiotapes)

Crannell, Kenneth. *Voice and Articulation.* Belmont, California: Wadsworth Publishing Company, second edition, 2000. (book and audiotapes)

Dale, Paulette Wainless, and Lillian Poms. *English Pronunciation for International Students.* Englewood Cliffs, New Jersey: Prentice Hall Regents, 1994. (book and audiotape)

Fragiadakis, Helen Kalkstein. *All Clear! Advanced Idioms and Pronunciation in Context.* Boston, Massachusetts: Heinle and Heinle, 1997.

Gilbert, Judy. *Clear Speech: Pronunciation and Listening Comprehension in North American English.* Cambridge: Cambridge University Press, second edition, 1993. (book and audiotape)

Grant, Linda. *Well Said: Advanced English Pronunciation.* Boston: Heinle and Heinle, 1993. (book and audiotape)

Lane, Linda. *Focus on Pronunciation: Principles and Practice for Effective Communication.* New York: Longman, 1993. (book and audiotape)

Makkai, Adam. *A Dictionary of American Idioms.* New York: Barrons, third edition, 1995.

Numrich, Carol. *Consider the Issues: Advanced Listening and Critical Thinking Skills.* New York: Longman, 1998. (book and audiotape)

Orion, Gertrude F. *Pronouncing American English: Sounds, Stress, and Intonation.* New York: Newbury House, second edition, 1998. (book and audiotape)

Pimsleur Speak and Read Essential English. Concord, Massachusetts: Simon and Schuster, 1998–2000. (audiotapes for native speakers of various languages, distributed by Heinle & Heinle Enterprises, Concord, Massachusetts)

Swan, Michael. *Practical English Usag*e. Oxford: Oxford University Press, second edition, 1995.

Wennerstrom, Ann. *Techniques for Teachers: A Guide for Nonnative Speakers of English.* Ann Arbor: The University of Michigan Press, 1991. (book and videotape)

Selected Books And Tapes On Teaching And The Culture Of The American Classroom

The Art of Discussion Leading: A Class with Chris Christensen. Cambridge, Massachusetts: The Derek Bok Center for Teaching and Learning, 1995. (videotape)

Church, Nancy, and Anne Moss. *How to Survive in the U.S.A.* New York: Cambridge University Press, 1983. (book and audiotape)

How to Speak: Lecture Tips from Patrick Winston. Cambridge, Massachusetts: The Derek Bok Center for Teaching and Learning, 1999. (videotape)

Ogami, Noriko, producer. *Cold Water.* Yarmouth, Maine: Intercultural Press, Inc., 1987. (videotape)

Race in the Classroom: The Multiplicity of Experience. Cambridge, Massachusetts: The Derek Bok Center for Teaching and Learning, 1992. (videotape)

Teaching in America: A Guide for International Faculty. Cambridge, Massachusetts: Derek Bok Center for Teaching and Learning, 1993. (videotape)

Thinking Together: Collaborative Learning in Science. Cambridge, Massachusetts: Derek Bok Center for Teaching and Learning, 1992. (videotape)

Women in the Classroom: Cases for Discussion. Cambridge, Massachusetts, The Derek Bok Center for Teaching and Learning, 1996. (videotape)

Index